Revisiting Construction
Second Edition

A look back at 10 years of college union projects

Association of College Unions International

Pictured on cover: Clarkson University's Student Center,
by Christopher F. Lenney

Copyright © 2012 by the Association of College Unions International

All rights reserved. No part of this book may be reproduced in any form or by any means, electronic or mechanical, including photocopying, recording, or by any storing and retrieval system, without written permission from the publisher.

Association of College Unions International
One City Centre, Suite 200
120 W. Seventh St.
Bloomington, IN 47404-3839 USA

ISBN-13: 978-0-923276-56-0
ISBN-10: 0-923276-56-4

Library of Congress Cataloging-in-Publication data available upon request.

This book is printed on acid- and lignin-free paper and meets all American National Standards for Informational Sciences standards for archival-quality paper.

Revisiting Construction

Second Edition

2002
Macalester College 9
DePaul University 10
Angelo State University 12
University of Colorado–Colorado Springs 13
University of Utah 14

2003
Austin Peay State University 19
Broome Community College 20
Bowling Green State University 21
California Polytechnic State University–
    San Luis Obispo 22
Sam Houston State University 23
San Diego State University 24
University of Chicago 25
University of Colorado–Boulder 26
University of Wisconsin–Madison 27
University of Wyoming 28
Davidson College 29

2004
Washington and Lee University 33
National University of Ireland–Cork 34
Bluffton College 35
The University of North Carolina–Greensboro 36
The Catholic University of America 37
University of Minnesota–Twin Cities 38
University of Arizona 39
State University of New York–Oneonta 40
University of Kansas 41
University of New Mexico 42
Southern Illinois University–Edwardsville 43
University of Manitoba 43
Colorado State University 44
Smith College 45

2005
Georgia Institute of Technology 50
The University of Alabama 51
St. Cloud State University 52
Arizona State University–East 53
Tulsa Community College–Southeast 54
University of Toronto 55
Allegheny College 56
Purdue University 57
Wartburg College 58
University of Dayton 59
Virginia Commonwealth University 60
University of North Dakota 61

2006
University of Minnesota–Crookston 66
Minnesota State University–Mankato 67
Creighton University 68
Appalachian State University 69
University of Maryland–College Park 70
University of Missouri–Rolla 71
University of Utah 72
College of Charleston 74
Wichita State University 75
Youngstown State University 76

2007
Christopher Newport University 82
Jacksonville University 83
University of Connecticut 84
California State University–Northridge 85
Colorado State University 86
Genesee Community College 87
Minnesota State University–Mankato 88
Philadelphia University 89
Phillips Exeter Academy 90
San Juan College 91
Southern Connecticut State University 92
Texas Tech University 93
University of North Carolina–Wilmington 94
Virginia Tech 95
Eastern Michigan University 96

A look back at 10 years of college union projects

2008
American University 101
California State University–Dominguez Hills 102
Fort Hays State University 103
Florida International University 104
University of Iowa 105
University of Utah 106
Vanderbilt University 107
University of Vermont 108
Virginia Commonwealth University 109
University of Wisconsin–River Falls 110

2009
Creighton University 115
Mississippi State University 116
University of Wisconsin–Parkside 117
Weber State University 118
Indiana University-Purdue University–Indianapolis 119
University of Texas–San Antonio 120
University of the Pacific 121
Edinboro University of Pennsylvania 122
Kalamazoo College 123
University of Wisconsin–Stevens Point 124
Northern Kentucky University 125

2010
Boise State Univeristy 129
Castleton State College 130
Curry College 131
University of Georgia 132
Iowa State University 133
Lawrence University 134
University of Maryland–College Park 135
Minnesota State University–Makato 136
University of North Carolina–Charlotte 137
University of North Florida 138
University of San Diego 139
University of South Florida 140
Texas A&M University–Commerce 141
Valparaiso University 142

2011
Clarkson University 147
University of Alabama 148
Armstrong Atlantic State University 149
Ball State University 150
University of Colorado 151
California State University–Channel Islands 152
California State University–Sacramento 153
University of Memphis 154
University of Missouri–Columbia 155
University of Missouri–Kansas City 156
The Ohio State University 157
Old Dominion University 158
University of Rochester 159
University of Southern California 160
State University of New York–New Paltz 161
Vanderbilt University 162
Winthrop University 163
University of Wisconsin–Superior 164
College of Wooster 165

2012
University of Connecticut 170
Coloardo College 172
Minnesota State University–Mankato 174
Normandale Community College 176
Rice University 178
University of South Florida 180
University of Texas–Austin 182
University of Wisconsin–Madison 184
Western Oregon University 185

Every year, higher education institutions around the world break ground on new college unions or begin the renovation process on already existing ones. Since 2002, ACUI has featured the completion of such projects at member institutions in the January *Bulletin*'s Renovation and Construction Showcase. This second edition of "Revisiting Construction" looks at featured projects from the past 10 years.

From large, public institutions to small, private colleges, "Revisiting Construction" offers the details on a variety of projects. Costs range from $100,000 to $136 million. Some institutions built brand new buildings and others completed smaller renovations.

While admiring the photos, take note of advancements made in the past 10 years. Keeping with current technology practices is a primary goal of several projects, but the desired advancements are different. Years ago, Ethernet jacks and new computer stations were needed. In 2012, unions are providing wireless Internet and installing gaming systems alongside flatscreen televisions.

An area of growth is a focus on sustainability. Buildings in earlier years occasionally incorporated water- or energy-saving features. In more recent years, however, both design and construction are sustainable. Several unions featured in "Revising Construction" achieved LEED certification for eco-friendly efforts.

A consistent detail throughout the years is student involvement. From initiating discussion on a new building to funding a renovation to choosing furniture, students are the driving force of nearly all the projects in this book.

Despite how large the building is, how much money was spent, or even what particular trend is seen in the design, there is one constant—unions remain "the community center of the college, serving students, faculty, staff, alumni, and guests," as stated in the Role of the College Union.

Please note that all information concerning institutions and unions on the following pages is as of the project completion date.

2002

Macalester College

DePaul University

Angelo State University

University of Colorado–Colorado Springs

University of Utah

■ Macalester College

renovation & construction showcase

Macalester College
Ruth Stricker Dayton Campus Center

St. Paul, Minn.

Submitted by: Brian Wagner, Director of Campus Programs/Center
Full-time equivalent enrollment: 1,835
Private, four-year, urban institution
Opened: February 2001
Total gross area: 70,000 sq. ft.
Source of funding: Private donations
Architects: Shepley Bulfinch Richardson and Abbott – Boston, Mass.
Facilities added or expanded: One lecture hall, seven meeting and seminar rooms, one atrium, one plaza, a performing arts stage, a student activities center with several offices for student organizations, one post office, one copy center, one convenience store, one dining facility, and one information desk

The Ruth Stricker Dayton Campus Center opened ahead of schedule in February 2001. The building was planned through a college-wide process involving students, faculty, and staff. The Campus Center is a gathering place for the campus community on a daily basis for food, conversation, activities, presentations, performances, and services. It also welcomes alumni, friends, and the larger community to campus.

The 268-seat John B. Davis Lecture Hall provides speakers with state-of-the-art equipment, including wireless Internet access as well as DVD, 16-millimeter slide, and video projection with a surround-sound environment.

An interesting skylight sculpture, created by James Carpenter, hangs in the atrium. Carpenter described the artwork. He said, "The skylight sculpture works with the phenomena of light and time to bring a constantly changing play of light into the Campus Center. When sunlight falls on the specially treated glass, half the spectrum is reflected and half passes through. The colors shift constantly, depending on the angle of the light and position of the viewer. ... Night lighting reflects the broad bands of color onto the interior surfaces of the ceiling with dramatic effect."

Café Mac, a 450-seat dining facility, operates four stations with freshly-prepared food. The Iron Grille is open all day. Diners can choose to sit in the open central area or in smaller "porches" along the windows. A faculty-staff dining room is located on the second floor.

DePaul University
Lincoln Park Student Center

Chicago, Ill.

Submitted by: Richard Thomas, Director of Student Centers
Full-time equivalent enrollment: 15,000
Private, four-year, urban institution
Total gross area: 150,000 sq. ft.
Percent of assignable space: 65%
Cost of project: $140 per sq. ft., not including FF&E, architectural/consultant fees, and other soft costs. Total project budget $25 million.
Source of funding: Institutional
Architects: WTW Architects – Pittsburgh, Pa.; VMC Architects – Chicago, Ill.
Facilities added: One ballroom/multipurpose room that is sub-dividable, two large meeting rooms, four medium meeting rooms, five small meeting rooms, four multipurpose lounges, an information center, a copy/print center, a video/pinball area, a cafeteria, a snack bar/fast food, another food service (catering bar and servery), coffeehouse, 10 departmental office suites, one billiards area (same as video/pinball area), one multicultural center, a private dining room, 26 e-mail stations, a spirit shop operated by bookstore to sell DePaul logo items, a chapel/reflection space, and a prayer room

Photos courtesy of DePaul University

The existing union, Stuart Center completed in 1972, was never completely adequate for DePaul, now the nation's largest Catholic university (as of 2002). In 1999, half of the Stuart Center was torn down to provide space to build an academic facility. This only exacerbated the situation. The building became little more than a cafeteria with some administrative office space for student affairs departments. There were only two meeting rooms and no space for retail or convenience services. Additionally, DePaul lacked adequate programming space—there was no auditorium or multipurpose room on campus that could hold more than 200 people for a program.

The new Lincoln Park Student Center is located much closer to the geographic center of the campus, making it

more accessible to a large percentage of the campus community. The design of the facility maximizes pedestrian traffic by creating a "Main Street" for DePaul with two first floor entrances located at major street intersections that serve to capture pedestrian sidewalk traffic and bring pedestrians inside the facility. It features significantly enhanced food service facilities, a coffee bar/cyber cafe, retail outlets including a copy shop and DePaul Spirit Shop, larger and more flexible meeting facilities, offices for student affairs departments, and a 400- to 600-seat multipurpose room.

The food service plan is developed in a marché style. The concept brings more of the food production out in front of the guest. This enhances the sensory experience as guests will see, smell, and hear the food being finished right in front of them and be able to customize it to their needs. The seating areas are integrated around these production platforms, eliminating the typical dining room separation. Each platform is outfitted with the equipment needed to produce particular menu items, ensuring that guests will have a wide variety of choices during each meal period. The cafeteria is the only university cafeteria on the Lincoln Park campus, serving both students on meal plans and other members of the campus community on a cash basis.

The coffee bar includes 20 computer terminals for students, faculty, and staff to use for checking e-mail, surfing the Internet, or logging onto the campus network. Additionally, numerous floor panels with electric power and Internet jacks are provided for those wishing to bring their own notebook computer. Lounges and cafeteria spaces throughout the building are "wired" with easy access to power and Internet capabilities in order to ensure "plug and play" possibilities in many locations.

Another noteworthy feature is that 20,000 square feet of space on the third floor is unprogrammed and only built out as a shell. When the original building program was completed, there were 2.5 floors of programmed space on the intended footprint of the building. The decision was made to build out a full third floor thus providing room to grow in the future.

Angelo State University
Houston Harte University Center

San Angelo, Texas

Submitted by: Rick E. Greig, Assistant Director, Programming
Full-time equivalent enrollment: 5,192
Public, four-year, urban institution
Opened: April 1972
Renovated: October 2000
Total gross area: 130,000 sq. ft.
Area added in renovation: 43,000 sq. ft.
Percent of assignable space: 56.2%
Cost of project: $77 per sq. ft.
Source of funding: 80% government, 10% private donations, and 10% institution
Architect: CZM Architects
Facilities added or expanded: One ballroom, 14 multipurpose rooms, one large meeting room, one medium meeting room, 14 small meeting rooms, one theater with fixed stage, two multipurpose lounges, one quiet/reading lounge, one television lounge, one art gallery, one information center, table tennis, billiards, games room, snack bar, seven offices, one outdoor plaza, one faculty lounge, one locker/check room, one bookstore, one graphics service, one post office, one credit union, and the West Texas Collection library/gallery

Before renovations, the building had electrical and plumbing problems, a lack of meeting space, a limited dining room area, outdated technology, and insufficient space for offices and student organizations. Approximately 25 students as well as staff and faculty were included in numerous focus groups to develop a survey of services needed by the building's users.

The renovation included improving the heating and cooling system. The new building is 25 percent more energy efficient than the old building. The new Ram Central Station also provides ample student organization office space. Large meeting rooms were designed for multiple uses as breakout rooms. Each meeting room has Internet-access capabilities. Furthermore, the technology in the project enhances learning through sound, audio-visual, satellite, teleconference, PowerPoint presentations, and Internet access.

In the process, students had direct input with color selections and furniture for office areas used by students.

Photos courtesy of University of Colorado–Colorado Springs

Colorado Springs, Colo.

Submitted by: Jeff C. Davis, Director of Operations and Management
Full-time equivalent enrollment: 5,533
Public, four-year, urban institution
Opened: 1976
Renovated: 1988 and August 2001
Total gross area: 90,361 sq. ft.
Area added in renovation: 8,276 sq. ft.
Percent of assignable space: 75–80%
Cost of project: $55.62 per sq. ft.
Source of funding: Student fees
Architect: H & L Architecture – Denver, Colo.
Facilities added or expanded: Two large meeting rooms, four medium meeting rooms, three small meeting rooms, one theater with fixed stage, one quiet/reading lounge, one television lounge, one information center, one copy/printer center, one pub, table tennis, games room, billiards, snack bar, four offices, two outdoor plazas, two locker/check rooms, one fitness room with aerobics room, one outdoor equipment area, and one bookstore

The campus had grown 30 percent in the last 10 years [1991–2001} and the facilities were in constant use and overuse. The University Center needed an upgrade in offered services, new space and design for clubs and organizations, and new, larger space for intramural and recreational sports along with expanded dining seating areas.

Student focus groups addressed the needs, including research on how much the students would be willing to pay in a student fee increase to fund the renovation project. All recognized student groups had representatives on focus groups. Student government officers served on the planning committee, and a University Center staff member served on the construction management committee.

In the renovation project, two sections of the existing University Center were joined via a two-story glass atrium/pavilion. The pavilion also connected the University Center to the secondary entrance to the Kraemer Family Library—the glass structure also visually brings these entities together. It brings together the academic heart of the campus and the heart of the out-of-classroom learning experience.

The project also brought many services to the University Center that were not available on campus previously, many of which are being eliminated at other campuses. Those services include a full-service games room, a pub, television lounge, convenience store, and enhanced sit-down food service.

University of Colorado–Colorado Springs
University Center

Photos courtesy of University of Utah

University of Utah
University of Utah Union

Salt Lake City, Utah

Submitted by: Whit Hollis, Director
Full-time equivalent enrollment: 22,486
Four-year, public, urban institution
Opened: 1957
Renovated: August 2001
Total gross area: 23,000 sq. ft.
Percent of assignable space: 76%
Cost of project: $10.96 per sq. ft.
Source of funding: Student fees
Architect: Gould Evans Associates – Salt Lake City

Not every institution has millions to spend on the construction or major renovation of the union. The University of Utah successfully reinvented the facility at an affordable cost. Since the remodeling projects, the number of people entering the building has doubled.

After developing a building analysis with the architect, the areas that needed changes were identified, all part of the new master plan for the building. The areas included in the renovation were selected as areas that would give the most impact to the union. The outdoor patio plaza had previously been used for reserved activities and functions, but sat empty during times when no activities were scheduled. The design and planning included providing tables and chairs fixed in place for students to use year round. Adirondack chairs were added so that students could move around and group as they want. The addition of propane space heaters has allowed the area to be used even in colder weather.

The lounge area at the ballroom corridor was designed to appear more like a "living room." Because students use this area to relax, study, and sleep, the furnishings needed to be more comfortable and inviting. The area has upholstered lounge chairs with tablet arms to support laptop computers and end tables with table lamps. Rocking chairs sit in front on large windows for students to enjoy the view. All furnishings, provided by ACUI Procure vendor High Point Furniture, are moveable so that as the master plan defines more appropriate areas for a student lounge, these furnishings can be relocated.

The remodeling of the north public corridor was the most dramatic change. The corridor, still in its original condition, was dark, unfriendly, and very plain. The corridor is the home to ASUU, Union Board, and *The Chronicle*, the campus newspaper. Sticking to a tight budget, corridor walls had windows added. Brick walls were covered with gyp board and painted white. Linoleum floors with bright colors and lively patterns were added. Ceiling light fixtures were replaced with brighter, more energy-efficient fixtures. New custom signage and benches added the finishing touches.

From start to finish, the project lasted three and a half months. A student, faculty, and staff committee began design planning after the budget was approved in May 2001. Planning ended in June, and the construction started the first of July. The projects were completed by the first day of school, Aug. 22, 2001, except for a few minor punch list items.

2003

Austin Peay State University

Broome Community College

Bowling Green State University

California Polytechnic State University–San Luis Obispo

Sam Houston State University

San Diego State University

University of Chicago

University of Colorado–Boulder

University of Wisconsin–Madison

University of Wyoming

Davidson College

Renovation & Construction SHOWCASE

Bartlett Hall, University of Chicago

Even as budgets in higher education became more tightly stretched, college unions continued constructing new and renovating old facilities to better serve their communities.

Austin Peay
State University
Morgan University Center
Clarksville, Tenn.

SUBMITTED BY: Andy Kean, Director
FULL-TIME EQUIVALENT ENROLLMENT: 5,173
FOUR-YEAR, PUBLIC INSTITUTION
UNION OPENED: 1968
REOPENED: March 2002
TOTAL GROSS AREA: 93,000 sq. ft.
PERCENT OF ASSIGNABLE SPACE: 60%
COST OF PROJECT: $13.2 million
SOURCE OF FUNDING: 100% student fees
ARCHITECTS: Lyle Cook Martin Architects – Clarksville, Tenn.
FACILITIES ADDED OR EXPANDED: A ballroom, two large meeting rooms, four small meeting rooms, a theater, three multipurpose lounges, two quiet/reading lounges, an information center, a cafeteria, a snack bar/fast food venue, a coffee house, six office spaces, an outdoor plaza/patio, a ticket office, a computer lab, billiards, a locker/check room, a faculty lounge, and two private dining rooms

The original Morgan University Center was built for a population of 2,000 students. Since then, the university more than doubled in size and the facility was not able to handle the volume of students. In 1995, students and staff began assessing the need for an expanded University Center. And in 1996, students voted to raise fees to cover the expense of a new building. For the next two and a half years, designs were developed. During that time, the design changed from adding onto the existing structure to demolishing it and building on the same footprint. Just prior to the project going to bid in January 1999, a tornado struck campus, damaging the University Center. Finally, almost a year later, the University Center was demolished and construction began.

Students were involved in the design phase through the selection of colors, and the project was totally funded by students, although many of them never actually got to see the project begin. But they believed in the concept and that it was important to invest in future students as others had done for them.

A wall of windows on the building's east and north sides highlights the lobby and eating areas. The coffeehouse has booths, Internet connections, and specially designed chairs that are a hit with students. The weekly performances on the stage there draw many on- and off-campus visitors to drink specialty coffees and enjoy the shows.

During the construction, students were without a union, and as a result, had a difficult time developing community. For three years, they met and had events in tents, outdoors, in the intramural facility, and in the cafeteria. While construction was going on, administrators could sense a lack of student focus and excitement about the university because there was no place to go for events, information sharing, or relaxing. But this year, they have seen a rise in school spirit that they directly attribute to the University Center.

Broome
Community College
BCC Ice Center
Binghamton, N.Y.

Photos courtesy of Broome Community College

SUBMITTED BY: Jesse Wells, Assistant to the Vice President of Student and Community Affairs
FULL-TIME EQUIVALENT ENROLLMENT: 3,667
TWO-YEAR INSTITUTION
UNION OPENED: 1958
ICE CENTER OPENED: November 2002
TOTAL GROSS AREA: 78,000 sq. ft.
AREA ADDED IN NEW CONSTRUCTION: 55,724 sq. ft.
PERCENT OF ASSIGNABLE SPACE: 78%
COST OF PROJECT: $9.6 million
SOURCE OF FUNDING: 50% state government; 50% county government
ARCHITECTS: The Hall Partnership – New York
FACILITIES ADDED: Ice rink, six locker rooms, a pro shop, a skate rental shop, an arcade and party room, and a café

Broome Community College's goal was to create a quality home for its varsity hockey team while providing a facility for community gatherings and events. The Ice Center includes a full-scale hockey rink with permanent seating for 775 people. Hallways inside connect the Ice Center with the existing Student Center building, one of the college's original five buildings.

The Ice Center provides local skating organizations (including youth and adult hockey teams and figure skating clubs) with ice time. Concerts, convocations, and other events also take place in the Ice Center. The first concert in the new rink sold out. More than 1,600 people visited campus in one day, which was a significant marketing benefit.

The Ice Center has also become a gathering place for students during lunch and common hour. Some attend open skate sessions while many get their lunch at the Blue Line Café or enjoy the arcade. And hockey games that were previously rarely attended are now full of people from the community, giving the college a chance to strengthen recruiting and introduce other college services to guests.

Bowling Green
State University

Bowen-Thompson Student Union
Bowling Green, Ohio

SUBMITTED BY: William Blain, Interim Director
FULL-TIME EQUIVALENT ENROLLMENT: 20,000
FOUR-YEAR, PUBLIC, RURAL INSTITUTION
UNION OPENED: 1958
REOPENED: January 2002
TOTAL GROSS AREA: 210,000 sq. ft.
AREA RENOVATED: 90,000 sq. ft.
AREA ADDED IN NEW CONSTRUCTION: 120,000 sq. ft.
PERCENT OF ASSIGNABLE SPACE: 65%
COST OF PROJECT: $35 million
SOURCE OF FUNDING: 97% student fees; 2% private donations; and 1% university
ARCHITECTS: The Collaborative Inc. – Toledo, Ohio; Perry, Dean, Rogers – Boston, Mass.
FACILITIES ADDED OR EXPANDED: A multipurpose room, two large meeting rooms, five medium-sized meeting rooms, five small meeting rooms, an auditorium, three multipurpose lounges, three quiet/reading lounges, a television lounge, an art gallery, an information center, a copy center, a food court, a pub, a coffee shop, two office suites, an outdoor patio, a computer lab, a multicultural center, a president's suite, eight e-mail stations, a bookstore, a Wendy's, a convenience store, and a student organization office suite

Students initiated interest and requested the renovation and expansion of the Bowen-Thompson Student Union. The 1958 union building was outdated, having little-used hotel space and bowling lanes, as well as a shortage of meeting rooms, program venues, and lounge spaces. Students served on the core construction committee and all sub-committees making decisions on aesthetics, furnishings, and food service choices.

The union now features daylight exposure to almost all spaces through large window areas and 22 skylights. The large central atrium space and unique configuration of the building are also noteworthy elements visitors enjoy. And there is a bold use of color throughout the union. The building's technology was also updated with the renovation and expansion, adding ethernet connections throughout the building and wireless connections in parts of the building and installing video projection capability in many meeting rooms.

California Polytechnic State University
San Luis Obispo

Julian A. McPhee University Union
San Luis Obispo, Calif.

SUBMITTED BY: Michelle Broom, Associated Students, Inc. Public Relations Coordinator
FULL-TIME EQUIVALENT ENROLLMENT: 17,000
FOUR-YEAR, PUBLIC, RURAL INSTITUTION
UNION OPENED: 1968
REOPENED: September 2002
TOTAL GROSS AREA: 102,000 sq. ft.
AREA RENOVATED: 4,500 sq. ft.
PERCENT OF ASSIGNABLE SPACE: 85%
COST OF PROJECT: $475,000
SOURCE OF FUNDING: Reserve funds from an auxiliary organization
ARCHITECTS: RRM Architects – San Luis Obispo, Calif.
FACILITIES ADDED: Nine new office spaces (there were 45 previously) and one medium-sized meeting room
FACILITIES RELOCATED TO THE EPICENTER: An art gallery with lounge, an information center, and a club resources area (which nearly tripled in size)

UNIVERSITY UNION epicenter

Associated Students, Inc. at Cal Poly conducted a referendum by which the students addressed the need for more programming (e.g., special events, concerts, outdoor adventures, and club programming). There was no place large enough in the union to accommodate all the services needed in one center. Based on advice from students via the University Union Advisory Board (UUAB), composed of students and two advisors, a site for the union was chosen and the design process started. The renovation and construction of the new "Epicenter" commenced in June 2002 and was ready to serve the students in September 2002.

Previously, there was no area in the union for club members to receive all of their programming needs in one place. Incorporating all of the services, from facility reservations to event planning, enabled staff to provide immediate service for all customers in a one-stop shop, the Epicenter. Beyond the one-stop shop, all union programs are now run from this one cohesive environment, providing for better communication, not only between full-time and student staff, but also between the staff and the customer. Also, new cordless phones were installed to increase the frontline staff's mobility and enable them to multi-task.

The comparatively minor renovation in one wing in the union created a facility to, among many things, fully manage and support clubs, plan student entertainment, and organize outdoor trips. In addition, the Epicenter was created with ease and accessibility in mind, and the environment is trendy and welcoming. A large foyer at the entrance has vaulted ceilings and natural light from full-wall windows. In addition, the unique spatial design includes a contemporary metal treatment with cool bold colors accented by recessed and track lighting. The space flows to a student art gallery complete with a lounge area.

Sam Houston State University

Lowman Student Center
Huntsville, Texas

SUBMITTED BY: Keri Rogers, Director of the Lowman Student Center and Student Activities
FULL-TIME EQUIVALENT ENROLLMENT: 13,000
FOUR-YEAR, PUBLIC INSTITUTION
UNION OPENED: April 1964
REOPENED: August 2002
TOTAL GROSS AREA: 144,000 sq. ft.
AREA RENOVATED: 128,081 sq. ft.
AREA ADDED IN NEW CONSTRUCTION: 15,919 sq. ft.
PERCENT OF ASSIGNABLE SPACE: 90,000 sq. ft.
COST OF PROJECT: $11 million
SOURCE OF FUNDING: 100% student fees
ARCHITECTS: Graeber, Simmons and Cowan – Austin, Texas
FACILITIES ADDED OR EXPANDED: A ballroom, three small meeting rooms, a television lounge, an information center, a fast food venue, another food service venue, a coffee house, and a private dining room

Before the renovation, the Lowman Student Center had roofing, HVAC, electrical, and plumbing problems, as well as outdated technology. Dining facilities were limited, and bookstore space was insufficient. A large multipurpose room was needed, as well as student organization work space and offices. Beginning in November 1997, a planning committee was organized to gather information and suggestions from members of the campus community about the programs, services, and facilities that might best serve the university's future needs. The planning committee also surveyed and collected information from various colleges and universities on college unions that had been recently built or renovated.

Students were involved at many steps in the process, including 1,100 who completed a needs assessment survey. Several design meetings and discussion sessions with the architects allowed for opinion assessment and further data gathering from students. Students voted to increase the Student Center fees, which financed the renovation project. Students had direct input with color selections and furniture. They also were offered tours of the Student Center throughout the entire renovation process.

The improvements to the Student Center were numerous. Building systems and technology (HVAC, sound, acoustics, etc.) were updated, including providing all meeting facilities with Internet access capabilities and enhanced learning through sound, audio-visual, satellite, teleconference, and computer presentations. The theater now has better accessibility and updated technology. A more spacious ballroom was built with a stage that provides for handicap accessibility and a loading dock. The games room was expanded and is now wired for the latest in computer virtual reality games and an updated sound system. More and specialized meeting rooms were developed, including a new multipurpose room. Dedicated student organization workspace and offices were constructed. The bookstore and food service options were expanded and enhanced. The theater, ballroom, games room, and dining areas are now directly accessible from the exterior. And a new two-story atrium allows for special programming and brings additional openness to the building.

San Diego State University

(Associated Students)
Aztec Recreation Center
San Diego, Calif.

SUBMITTED BY: Eric Huth, Campus Recreation Director
FULL-TIME EQUIVALENT ENROLLMENT: 33,391
FOUR-YEAR, PUBLIC INSTITUTION
UNION OPENED: July 1997
REOPENED: August 2002
TOTAL GROSS AREA: 76,500 sq. ft.
AREA RENOVATED: 18,000 sq. ft.
AREA ADDED IN NEW CONSTRUCTION: 500 sq. ft.
ASSIGNABLE SPACE: 72,000 sq. ft.
COST OF PROJECT: $1.2 million
SOURCE OF FUNDING: $78,000 from Associated Students Future Facilities; $1.2 million from state-held SDSU Student Union Surplus Revenue Fund
ARCHITECT: Mosher, Drew, Watson and Ferguson – San Diego
FACILITIES ADDED OR EXPANDED: Nine administrative offices, a small conference room, vending machines, a laundry room, two information centers, a television lounge, a computer station (with six computers), and a 200-square-foot massage therapy studio

The Associated Students at San Diego State University is the only auxiliary in the nation to operate an on-campus recreation-fitness facility on a regular 24-hours-a-day, five-days-per-week schedule. The Aztec Recreation Center program serves SDSU's students, faculty, staff, alumni, and the surrounding community. The Aztec Recreation Center is the host of most of Associated Students Campus Recreation-based programs, including intramural sports, special events, weight training, massage therapy, personal training, sports clubs, noncredit-based classes, informal recreation, martial arts, group cycling, indoor rock climbing, fitness/wellness activities, and group fitness classes.

As a result of the success of these programs, it was increasingly difficult to serve the customers and provide superior services. Administrative space was totally inadequate requiring the use of conference space and storage areas to accommodate staff. The laundry equipment could not handle the increasing volume of members and maintain the desired level of customer service. The front entrance needed to be remodeled to handle the traffic and improve disabled access. Therefore, the Associated Students of SDSU commissioned the architectural firm of Mosher, Drew, Watson and Ferguson to study the existing operations and programs to provide SDSU with a cost estimate and plan for renovation.

Before the remodel, SDSU students let planners know this proposal was important. Increased member satisfaction and retention was a natural by-product of this expansion. SDSU students see the expansion as further proof that the Associated Students cares about offering superior service and exceeding their expectations.

These students understand that an enhanced quality of life and educational experience is provided to them with outstanding facilities, programs, and services. The Aztec Recreation Center and other campus recreation facilities are operated under a voluntary membership-based revenue plan that generates 97 percent of the annual operating revenue needed to fund the $3.5 million program. The revenue from monthly membership fees varies for students ($14 per month), alumni, faculty-staff ($21 per month), and members of the community ($31 per month).

Photos courtesy of University of Chicago

University of Chicago

Bartlett Hall
Chicago

SUBMITTED BY: Curt Heuring, University Architect
FULL-TIME EQUIVALENT ENROLLMENT: 21,641
FOUR-YEAR, PRIVATE, URBAN INSTITUTION
UNION OPENED: 1904
REOPENED: January 2002
TOTAL GROSS AREA: 66,260 sq. ft.
AREA RENOVATED: 64,000 sq. ft.
AREA ADDED IN NEW CONSTRUCTION: 2,260 sq. ft.
PERCENT OF ASSIGNABLE SPACE: 80%
COST OF PROJECT: $13.5 million
SOURCE OF FUNDING: Institution
ARCHITECTS: Bruner/Cott & Associates Inc.
FACILITIES ADDED OR EXPANDED: A multipurpose room, a large meeting room, two theaters, a multipurpose lounge, a quiet/reading lounge, an information center, a 550-seat cafeteria, three offices, a ticket office, a campus market, and six student organization offices

Bartlett Hall was originally conceived as the United States Olympic Team men's training facility. The three-story, limestone structure was built in 1904 and served as the University of Chicago's athletics department for nearly a century. But as part of a campus-wide master plan, the concept for a new athletic center was developed, leaving Bartlett Gymnasium without a use. With the construction of a 750-room residence hall adjacent to Bartlett Hall, and the planned demise of another on-campus dining facility, Bartlett made perfect sense as a location for additional dining and a college union.

Student focus groups and surveys also identified the needs for new social and classroom spaces, out of which came the new twin theater rehearsal and dance performance areas and the student lounge and organization offices.

The renovation of Bartlett Hall was to blend new amenities and facilities with the building's historic look and character. The basement floor was excavated and lowered nearly 36 inches to accommodate 350 tons of new heating and air conditioning systems. A comprehensive salvage program allowed "harvesting" of much of the original, 100-year-old limestone for use in repairing the existing structure and matching new stone. Additional materials saved and reused included the wooden gymnasium floor, iron and oak doors, and other period artifacts. The original diamond-paned windows were replicated using new double-glazed, energy-efficient glass with laminated lead caming. The suspended running track now serves as an observation deck and cozy lounge area, offering dramatic views of campus. And perhaps the hall's "highlight" is its new energy-efficient, full-length skylight that fills the space with sunshine.

25

Photos courtesy of University of Colorado–Boulder

University of Colorado–Boulder
University Memorial Center
Boulder, Colo.

SUBMITTED BY: Carlos Garcia, University Memorial Center Director
FULL-TIME EQUIVALENT ENROLLMENT: 26,000
PUBLIC INSTITUTION
UNION OPENED: 1953
REOPENED: September 2002
TOTAL GROSS AREA: 262,869 sq. ft.
AREA RENOVATED: 160,000 sq. ft.
AREA ADDED IN NEW CONSTRUCTION: 50,700 sq. ft.
PERCENT OF ASSIGNABLE SPACE: 73%
COST OF PROJECT: $27 million
SOURCE OF FUNDING: 100% student fees
ARCHITECTS: Gensler Inc. – Denver, Colo.; WTW Architects, Inc. – Pittsburgh, Pa.
FACILITIES ADDED OR EXPANDED: A multipurpose room, nine large meeting rooms, 11 medium-sized meeting rooms, eight small meeting rooms, a multipurpose lounge, a television lounge, an art gallery, an information center, a copy center, a nightclub, 10 bowling lanes, four fast-food venues, two outdoor terraces, an office area, a computer lab, eight billiards tables, a multicultural center, a locker/check room, 22 e-mail stations, and a bookstore

Opened in 1953, the University Memorial Center underwent a major renovation and expansion in 1964 when 50,000 square feet were added. Since that time, the student body had nearly doubled in size and many programs and student groups had been turned away for lack of space.

Once the concept of an expansion/renovation was agreed upon, University Memorial Center administration began a series of focus groups and public forums with representatives from campus cost centers, off-campus users, and student groups to determine needs. The resultant addition addressed concerns for additional student group space, more retail offerings, more light, and an expanded bookstore. One of the most stunning architectural aspects of the new addition is the five-story atrium. All office space and conference rooms are now "technologically smart," equipped to handle telecommunications, computer needs, and audio-visual needs. One of the new entertainment features added is the renovated nightclub, Club 156, which provides students with nonalcoholic weekend and evening entertainment alternatives.

The University Memorial Center Board, comprised of students, faculty, and staff, initiated the expansion and played a key role in promoting the idea to the University of Colorado Student Union legislative council. They supplied the information for the needs feasibility study and launched a marketing campaign to get the project ratified by the students. In addition, graduating seniors donated money to the development of a commuter lounge.

One of the most noteworthy aspects of the project was to develop a building that was "green." The building follows a new architectural trend to "design for recycling." This trend emphasizes creating space for the storage and collection of recycling; such as, the new University Memorial Center has built-in recycling collection cabinets and 30 percent more space for the storage of recyclables. The building also used literally tons of recycled material, including floor tile and carpeting. During construction, the center was able to recycle more than 400 tons of concrete, 1,102 pounds of copper, and 36 tons of steel. Even sinks, drains, and toilettes were recycled.

University of Wisconsin–Madison
Memorial Union
Madison, Wis.

SUBMITTED BY: Richard Pierce, Assistant Director of Facilities
FULL-TIME EQUIVALENT ENROLLMENT: 45,000
FOUR-YEAR, PUBLIC, URBAN INSTITUTION
UNION OPENED: October 1928
REOPENED: October 2002
AREA RENOVATED: 3,400 sq. ft.
PERCENT OF ASSIGNABLE SPACE: 100%
COST OF PROJECT: $400,000
SOURCE OF FUNDING: $300,000 from private donations; $100,000 from department operating funds
ARCHITECTS: Strang Partners – Madison, Wis.
FACILITY RENOVATED: Main Lounge

Memorial Union's Main Lounge had been a primary gathering space for the university community and the site of many events of significance to the campus. However, it had been nearly 40 years since the space was last extensively refurbished, and previously there had never been adequate ventilation, heating control, or air conditioning, making the room virtually unusable during severe weather months. To restore the room's luster and make it again a destination location for major campus events, a complete restoration was undertaken.

Never-before-available climate controls and air conditioning were installed in a manner sensitive to the space's elaborate interior. Original hand-painted stencils, which previously had been painted over, were documented and replicated. Original plaster moldings, thought to have been previously removed, were uncovered, incorporated into a revised ceiling plan, and restored to original detail. And the original ivory and gold patterned terrazzo flooring was fully restored.

Students' input was solicited through focus groups during the initial planning phase and in the selection of interior finishes and furnishings. Student committees also reviewed space-use policies and coordinated art installations.

The costs of the project were underwritten by the UW Class of 1950. Those alumni see themselves as the first class to benefit from the G.I. Bill and wanted to give back to their alma mater something the university community could enjoy in years to come.

University of Wyoming

Wyoming Union
Laramie, Wyo.

SUBMITTED BY: Charlie Francis, Director
FULL-TIME EQUIVALENT ENROLLMENT: 8,666
FOUR-YEAR, PUBLIC INSTITUTION
UNION OPENED: 1938
REOPENED: September 2002
TOTAL GROSS AREA: 126,484 sq. ft.
AREA RENOVATED: 95,819 sq. ft.
AREA ADDED IN NEW CONSTRUCTION: 16,732 sq. ft.
PERCENT OF ASSIGNABLE SPACE: 62%
COST OF PROJECT: $11.1 million
SOURCE OF FUNDING: 95% student fees; 5% bookstore
ARCHITECTS: GSG Architecture – Casper, Wyo.
FACILITIES ADDED OR EXPANDED: A ballroom, two large meeting rooms, five multipurpose lounges, two television lounges, an art gallery, an information center, a copy center, a pub, four fast-food venues, three other food service areas, seven office space suites, three outdoor plazas or patios, a ticket office, a computer lab, a billiards area, a poster and graphics service center, three e-mail stations, a bookstore, a student publications office, a student technical services office, a student attorney office, an adult student center/women's center, and a multicultural resource center

Photos courtesy of University of Wyoming

The last major renovation/addition to the Wyoming Union was in 1972. By 1998, the needs of the campus had changed dramatically. Focus groups were formed across campus, consisting of students, faculty, administrators, and staff. Support for an improved and updated facility was strong throughout the university and state. The University of Wyoming is the only public four-year university in the state, and therefore enjoys a unique relationship with the citizens of Wyoming.

Representatives from Associated Students of the University of Wyoming and the Union Board were part of the design team. All student organizations housed in the union were able to enumerate their needs for all aspects of their office space. During the renovation process, the students were kept apprised of the project's progress.

The most noteworthy features of the Wyoming Union renovation are the three fireplaces in different parts of the building. Funded solely by Associated Students of the University of Wyoming, these fireplaces serve as the focal points of informal gathering areas and lounges. The Wyoming Family Room, adjacent to the Yellowstone Ballroom, was formerly a storage area but has been transformed into a large meeting space with numerous windows overlooking the central area of campus. The flooring throughout the building is a neutral porcelain tile, with the lower level funded by the President's Office. The new food court area consists of four branded food concepts, adding a variety of food choices that were previously unavailable to the university community.

Photos courtesy of Davidson College

Davidson College

**Knobloch Campus Center
Davidson, N.C.**

SUBMITTED BY: William Brown, Union Director
FULL-TIME EQUIVALENT ENROLLMENT: 1,600
FOUR-YEAR, PRIVATE INSTITUTION
UNION OPENED: August 2001
TOTAL GROSS AREA: 122,000 sq. ft.
COST OF PROJECT: $25 million
SOURCE OF FUNDING: Private donations
ARCHITECTS: MacLachlan, Cornelius, and Filoni – Pittsburgh, Pa.
FACILITIES ADDED OR EXPANDED: A multipurpose room, a large meeting room, a medium-sized meeting room, four small meeting rooms, a theater, a multipurpose lounge, a television lounge, an information center, a copy center, a pub, a table tennis area, a snack bar/fast food venue, 30 offices, two outdoor plazas, a ticket office, a computer lab, a billiards area, a fitness equipment room, a poster/graphics service center, an outdoor equipment area, 11 e-mail stations, and a bookstore

Davidson has had three other unions in 50 years and finally got it right with the Knobloch Campus Center, a project that took more than 15 years to complete from its inception in 1985. The college wrestled with concepts for a long time, sometimes scrapping the project completely. There were three planning committees—1988, 1993, and 1996–2001. Students were on every planning committee, sometimes being in the majority. Students helped in every way, from participating in site visits at other campuses to testing furniture prior to purchase. The student body as a whole helped a great deal in responding to surveys and attending focus groups. Three different surveys, the work and report of a planner, the focus groups, and the site visits helped Davidson determine their needs.

Were those needs met? Absolutely. In the end, nothing the planning committee determined necessary was omitted.

Students love the place and spend a large portion of their time there. The union is built around a three-story atrium with a skylight. The entire space is people-friendly and the program venues are excellent. The multipurpose room/pub is named for C. Shaw Smith, longtime director of the Davidson College Union and former ACUI president. The Duke Family Performance Hall is a 600-seat, state-of-the-art performance hall that was host to the Royal Shakespeare Company for the hall's opening in February 2002.

2004

Washington and Lee University
National University of Ireland–Cork
Bluffton College
The University of North Carolina–Greensboro
The Catholic University of America
University of Minnesota–Twin Cities
University of Arizona
State University of New York–Oneonta
University of Kansas
University of New Mexico
Southern Illinois University–Edwardsville
University of Manitoba
Colorado State University
Smith College

RENOVATION & CONSTRUCTION showcase

As college campuses continue to grow and the tastes of students become more eclectic, the union must play a major role in recruitment and retention by facilitating a gathering space that serves diverse interests. In 2004, though budgets were tight and the economy left much to be desired, many college unions across the world celebrated the completion of their building's renovation or construction project, helping them better meet their communities' needs.

In preparing for reaccreditation in the 1980s, Washington and Lee faculty, staff, and students concerned with creating a stronger sense of community and shared institutional identity recommended the construction of a centrally located University Commons. The guiding principle in all deliberations from then on was to create a focal point for community life to offset fragmentation of the student body by greek affiliations and upperclassmen living off campus.

The new centrally located University Commons has enabled Washington and Lee to be a purely pedestrian campus. It fits with the campus's traditional architecture and brings inside the natural beauty of the Shenandoah Valley. A boardwalk provides handicap access from the nearby parking deck and offers the sensation of walking through the trees in the ravine that borders the building on one side. Another feature is an underground service dock accessed by a tunnel from the street. This detail allowed the architects to design a building with four fronts and no backdoor, no visible dumpsters, generators, or exposed equipment.

WASHINGTON AND LEE UNIVERSITY

JOHN W. ELROD UNIVERSITY COMMONS
LEXINGTON, VA.

SUBMITTED BY: Leroy C. Atkins II, Acting Director
FULL-TIME EQUIVALENT ENROLLMENT: 2,100
FOUR-YEAR, PRIVATE, RURAL INSTITUTION
OPENED: September 2003
TOTAL AREA: 85,000 sq. ft.
ASSIGNABLE SPACE: 61%
COST OF PROJECT: $30 million
SOURCE OF FUNDING: 100% private donations
ARCHITECT: VMDO Architects, P.C. – Charlottesville, Va.
NEW FACILITIES: Four multipurpose rooms, two large meeting rooms, five medium-sized meeting rooms, four small meeting rooms, two dining venues, a bookstore, a crafts center, three music learning lounges, a theater, and an auditorium

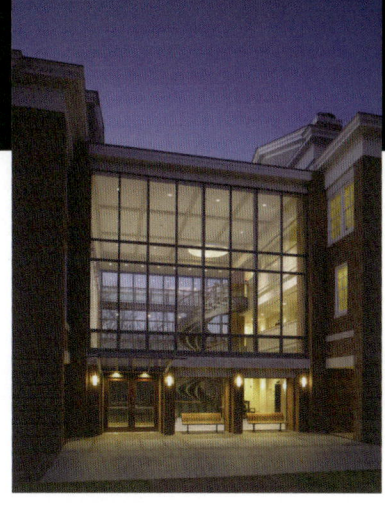

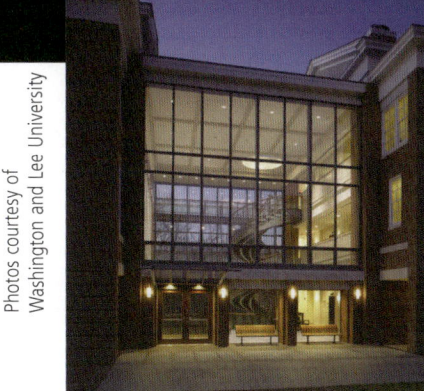

Photos courtesy of Washington and Lee University

NATIONAL UNIVERSITY OF IRELAND–CORK

ARAS NA MAC LEINN
CORK, IRELAND

SUBMITTED BY: Liz Carroll, Facility Services Manager
FULL-TIME EQUIVALENT ENROLLMENT: 14,000
FOUR-YEAR, PUBLIC, URBAN INSTITUTION
OPENED: 1996
REOPENED: February 2003
TOTAL AREA: 4,500 sq. meters
AREA ADDED: 2,500 sq. meters
PERCENT OF ASSIGNABLE SPACE: 68%
COST OF PROJECT: $6.5 million (U.S.)
SOURCE OF FUNDING: 50% student fees; 50% institution
ARCHITECT: O'Riordan Staehli Architects – Cork, Ireland
FACILITIES ADDED: Lounge space, two large meeting rooms (fully equipped with audio-visual facilities), a computer room, three office spaces, an e-bar, a food-service area, two café bars, an outdoor plaza, a bookstore, and a bank

In 2000, a survey to determine student and staff priorities indicated a need for expanded lounge spaces and enhancement of the coffee shop plus full catering facilities in National University of Ireland–Cork's union. The construction and expansion took two years to complete. During this time, the original facility and services continued to operate.

The new extension's architecture is expressed as a series of simple sculptural forms—light, scale, and material expression. The southern edge of the extension has been conceived as an atrium, an entirely glass structure that not only provides interconnection of the social spaces, but also is an important device for ventilating much of the building.

Following a recent traffic count, the number of customers using the building daily is up almost 30 percent, at an average of 11,000 per day. Donnchadh Ó hAodha, general manager of the center, said the figures clearly demonstrate the popularity and real value of the services and social opportunities the completed project helps offer to the campus community.

BLUFFTON COLLEGE
MARBECK CENTER
BLUFFTON, OHIO

SUBMITTED BY: Mark Bourassa, Director of Marbeck Center and Conferences
FULL-TIME EQUIVALENT ENROLLMENT: 1,100
FOUR-YEAR, PRIVATE, RURAL INSTITUTION
OPENED: March 1968
ADDITION OPENED: March 2003
EXISTING AREA: 37,000 sq. ft.
AREA RENOVATED: 2,700 sq. ft.
AREA ADDED: 6,300 sq. ft.
TOTAL GROSS AREA: 43,300 sq. ft.
ASSIGNABLE SPACE: 80%
COST OF PROJECT: $2 million
SOURCE OF FUNDING: 100% private donations
ARCHITECT: Rooney, Clinger, Murray Architects – Findlay, Ohio
FACILITIES ADDED OR EXPANDED: A snack shop, a games room, banquet/meeting rooms, a multipurpose room, computer lab space, student-designated programming space, and lounge space

The project initially was limited to updating the Marbeck Center snack shop; however, the greater need for a place to hang out on campus existed. The planning committee was made up almost entirely of students. Students were actively involved in the design process and in selecting the colors, fabrics, carpet, and furniture. They even helped name the facility.

Students' recommendations included: a stage area, now the primary programming area on campus; a games room to help make the center a campus "hang out"; and a banquet/meeting room that has become the most reserved room in Marbeck Center. The college also had just opened a technology-laden academic building, so there was a strong desire to meet the standards set by that facility.

Through a complete renovation and addition to the original snack shop, now called "Bob's Place," student traffic and activities have risen to new levels and Bob's Place has become the place to be. Bob's Place offers a big-screen projection system, computers with wireless access, and a games room. The snack shop did more business in the three weeks after the reopening than during the entire previous year.

THE UNIVERSITY OF NORTH CAROLINA–GREENSBORO

ELLIOTT UNIVERSITY CENTER
GREENSBORO, N.C.

SUBMITTED BY: Bruce Michaels, Assistant Vice Chancellor
FULL-TIME EQUIVALENT ENROLLMENT: 12,350
FOUR-YEAR, PUBLIC INSTITUTION
UNION OPENED: 2001
REOPENED: January 2003
TOTAL AREA: 189,635 sq. ft.
ASSIGNABLE SPACE: 61%
COST OF PROJECT: $23 million
SOURCE OF FUNDING: 65% student fees; 2% private donations; 33% vendors
ARCHITECT: Walter Robbs Callahan & Pierce – Winston-Salem, N.C.
FACILITES ADDED OR EXPANDED: A ballroom, three multipurpose rooms, two large meeting rooms, eight medium meeting rooms, seven small meeting rooms, an auditorium (fixed seats), three multipurpose lounges, two quiet/reading lounges, a television lounge, an art gallery, an information center, a video/pinball room, a snack bar/fast food area, another food service venue, a coffee house, three outdoor plazas/patios, a ticket/box office, a billiards area, a multicultural center, a photo dark room, a locker/check room, a poster/graphics service, an e-mail station, a bookstore, and a meditation room

Located at a key pedestrian crossroads on campus, the Elliott University Center has been literally and symbolically identified as the University of North Carolina–Greensboro's center since it opened in 1953. Gradually, the university community outgrew the center, and since 1984 various studies have explored building a new facility as well as renovating and expanding the existing building. A significant challenge was to find a solution that would limit the financial burden on students. Open forums were held with the architects for students to provide input with the design process, and student organizations participated in design development and review. The end project is an example of what can be done to successfully transform an antiquated building.

This long-anticipated renovation provides more useful spaces, improved appearance, and better traffic circulation to support the community well into the future. The new center now has a multipurpose ballroom, an auditorium seating 481, and 19 meeting rooms, all with state-of-the-art technology. Specialty spaces include a multicultural resource center, meditation center, and art gallery. The renovated facility also houses the Student Activities Center, with meeting and office space for affiliated student organizations.

Photos courtesy of University of North Carolina–Greensboro

THE CATHOLIC UNIVERSITY OF AMERICA
EDWARD J. PRYZBYLA UNIVERSITY CENTER
WASHINGTON, D.C.

SUBMITTED BY: Bill Jonas, Director, University Center, Student Programs and Events
FULL-TIME EQUIVALENT ENROLLMENT: 4,535
FOUR-YEAR, PRIVATE, URBAN INSTITUTION
OPENED: March 2003
TOTAL AREA: 104,000 sq. ft.
ASSIGNABLE SPACE: 65%
COST OF PROJECT: $27 million
SOURCE OF FUNDING: 61% tax-exempt bond; 39% private donations
ARCHITECT: Bohlin Cywinski Jackson – Wilkes-Barre, Pa.
FACILITIES ADDED: A large multipurpose space, four medium-sized meeting rooms, five small meeting rooms, three lounge spaces, an information center, a bookstore, two dining facilities, a convenience store, four office suites, a student organization resource room, eight student organization storage closets, 10 student organization offices, an ATM, six computer kiosks, and an outdoor seating/programming space

Although the use of brick in building the Edward J. Pryzbyla University Center tie it to the rest of the campus, its steel and glass features make it stand out as a truly unique facility. The use of glass has been so extensive that some have called the union a "beacon" after nightfall on the campus. The exposed concrete columns, steel beams, ductwork, and other functional building elements also add to the architecture's drama, as does one of its main features, the three-level atrium that creates a central core of the building while also allowing air to circulate and light to reach each level.

On a practical note, the new facility incorporates energy-saving measures, such as an ice-making/storage system. Through the new system, ice is made during the night and then used during the day for cooling.

UNIVERSITY OF MINNESOTA– TWIN CITIES

COFFMAN MEMORIAL UNION
MINNEAPOLIS, MINN.

SUBMITTED BY: Karen Lyons, Assistant Director/Director of Marketing
FULL-TIME EQUIVALENT ENROLLMENT: 46,000
FOUR-YEAR, PUBLIC, URBAN INSTITUTION
OPENED: 1940
REOPENED: January 2003
TOTAL AREA: 350,328 sq. ft.
ASSIGNABLE SPACE: 87.5%
COST OF PROJECT: $71.5 million
SOURCE OF FUNDING: 68% student fees; 32% institution
ARCHITECT: Ellerbe-Becket – Minneapolis, Minn.
FACILITIES ADDED: A ballroom/auditorium, more than 75 offices, 10 multipurpose lounges, two multipurpose rooms, two large meeting rooms, six medium-sized meeting rooms, seven small meeting rooms, two food service areas including a food court with eight fast food venues, a deli, a coffee venue, a games room with 12 billiards tables and 14 bowling lanes, a locker rental area, a private faculty/staff/membership club with a bar, an information center/ticket outlet, a computer lab, a copy center, a theater, an auditorium, eight e-mail stations, a television lounge, four outdoor patios, two green spaces, an entire floor dedicated to student organizations and cultural centers, an art gallery/reception room, a convenience store, a travel service, a security monitor station, and a bank

Photos by Brian Droege

According to a 1998 survey, Coffman was not providing seven of the top 10 services students wanted in their union: short-term parking, a bookstore, air conditioning (making it a nine-month facility because of 100-degree temperatures), computer lab, quiet lounge space, national- and local-brand food choices, and a first-run movie theater. The theater features only second-run films, but all other services were realized. In addition, Coffman's infrastructure was upgraded to comply with codes and ADA regulations.

A parking garage was transformed into a 40,000-square-foot bookstore and a 400-seat theater. Original art deco features were restored, including terrazzo flooring and the return of a fireplace that was removed during a 1970s renovation. The main first floor entrance doors were also brought back to allow for easier access to the building. Escalators were installed to improve traffic flow. The building is also the first on campus with full wireless computer network capabilities.

When planning began, students and staff visited unions across the United States that were recently or in the process of being renovated or built. Feedback was solicited from focus groups and public meetings. When plans to improve the union were first discussed, it was proposed that Coffman be torn down, but students and alumni rallied to save the building, just like students in the 1930s rallied to construct the building.

UNIVERSITY OF ARIZONA
STUDENT UNION MEMORIAL CENTER
TUCSON, ARIZ.

SUBMITTED BY: Bonnie Arriaga, Office Supervisor, Center for Student Involvement and Leadership
FULL-TIME EQUIVALENT ENROLLMENT: 36,000
FOUR-YEAR, PUBLIC INSTITUTION
OPENED: January 2003
TOTAL AREA: 405,000 sq. ft.
ASSIGNABLE SPACE: 72%
COST OF PROJECT: $60 million
SOURCE OF FUNDING: 94% institution; 6% private donations
ARCHITECT: MHTN Architects – Salt Lake City
FACILITIES ADDED: 50 office spaces, seven large meeting rooms, four medium-sized meeting rooms, 12 small meeting rooms, 10 multipurpose rooms, a multicultural center, an information center, a computer lab, a poster/graphics service, an art gallery, a bookstore, a television lounge, a multipurpose lounge, six quiet/reading lounges, eight outdoor spaces, a cafeteria, two coffee houses, four other food service areas, a private dining room, six fast food venues, a locker/coat check area, a ballroom, a theater (fixed stage), a ticket office, a billiards area, a table tennis area, a video/pinball games area, and an outdoor equipment area

The Memorial Student Union was facing maintenance, repair, space, and ADA compliance challenges. The interior had been upgraded, but the potential of the mechanical infrastructure failing was high and the need to do a major building project was apparent.

Students initiated a referendum effort, and although it failed, it provided energy for student and university leaders to look for other sources to fund the building project.

The demolition of the original building and erection of the new building took place in the footprint of the original structure while the union remained open to the public at all times. Multiple moves of dining, facilities, programming, and business operations were made by the union staff on weekends or overnight. The Student Union Memorial Center also continued reservation and facility services when it had no rooms to offer. The staff researched available rooms across campus and continued to serve customers as a one-stop-shop for catering and events.

STATE UNIVERSITY OF NEW YORK–ONEONTA

CHARLES W. HUNT COLLEGE UNION
ONEONTA, N.Y.

SUBMITTED BY: Robb Ryan Q. Thibault, Director, Charles W. Hunt College Union
FULL-TIME EQUIVALENT ENROLLMENT: 5,500
FOUR-YEAR, PUBLIC INSTITUTION
OPENED: September 1972
REOPENED: October 2003
TOTAL AREA: 71,799 sq. ft.
AREA RENOVATED: 21,400 sq. ft.
ASSIGNABLE SPACE: 71%
COST OF PROJECT: $1.1 million
SOURCE OF FUNDING: 65% government; 35% auxiliary service revenue
ARCHITECT: David Smotrich & Partners LLP – New York City
FACILITIES ADDED: A theater, six office spaces, and a medium-sized event space

Despite infrastructure improvements made in the Hunt Union in its 30 years, as well as changes in the services provided, there was interest in a renovation. A committee of students, faculty, and staff was formed, and a consultant was hired to study the union. A phone survey of students was conducted to assess interest in services, and input from student groups and other organizations was sought throughout the project.

The addition of a 125-seat theater—which shows current films and offers an alternative space for classes and mid-sized events—and the scaling down of a small stage venue created two spaces, where one space had existed. Renovation of the historic "rathskeller" increased room capacity by 28 percent and added a fireplace, sound system, and lighting, transforming it to serve as a performance space. The relocation of student office space, commingled with the activity areas, also raised awareness of Student Association functions.

Two of the most dramatic new features are the entrance on the lower level, which includes a metal curvilinear ceiling and new lighting, and an expanded stairwell that creates an attractive, visual connection between levels.

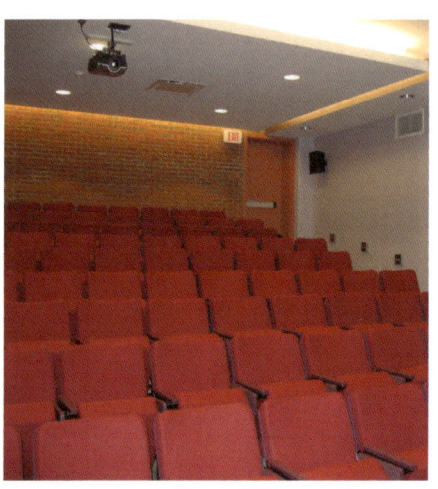

UNIVERSITY OF KANSAS
KU MEMORIAL UNIONS
LAWRENCE, KAN.

SUBMITTED BY Thomas Patrick Beard, Building Services Director, KU Memorial Unions
FULL-TIME EQUIVALENT ENROLLMENT: 28,000
FOUR-YEAR, PUBLIC INSTITUTION
OPENED: 1927
PROJECT COMPLETED: 1989, 1993, 2003 (three phases)
EXISTING AREA: 225,000 sq. ft.
AREA RENOVATED: 6,500 sq. ft.
AREA ADDED: 17,500 sq. ft.
TOTAL AREA: 232,500 sq. ft.
ASSIGNABLE AREA: 78%
COST OF PROJECT: $6.3 million
SOURCE OF FUNDING: 89% student fees; 11% union internal funds
ARCHITECT: Gould Evans & Associates – Lawrence, Kan.
FACILITIES ADDED OR EXPANDED: A multipurpose room, three outdoor gathering spaces, an information center, 19 student office spaces, two staff offices, a medium-sized meeting room, two small meeting rooms, a fast food venue, a dining space, a table service dining area, a coffee house, a bookstore, a video/pinball area, a billiards table area, and an engraving service

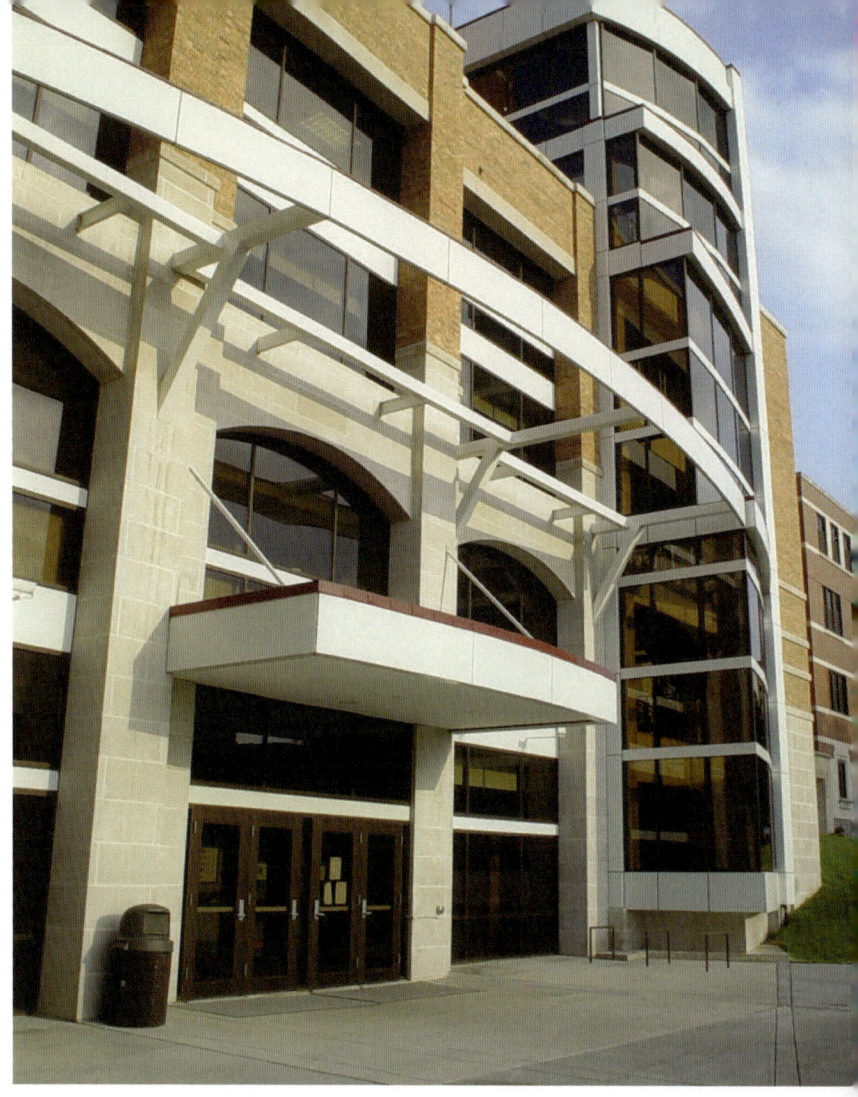

To meet growing needs for enlarged student organization space and centralized conveniences, union expansion was necessary. Each step in the project was taken before the planning committee (50 percent of whose members were students), and each plan was taken before the student body for review and comment prior to approval.

Improvements included a 70 percent increase in student organization space. Also, the bookstore was relocated to an area where formerly a road ran under the building. And a walkway connecting a parking garage to the union turned out to have been a major enhancement in terms of perceived convenience to union users, although it was almost an afterthought during planning.

A new centralized stairwell has a predominately glass feature, allowing sunlight on all levels. At its base is a large, native limestone bench engraved with "ROCK CHALK JAYHAWK, KU." On the ceiling is a lighted painting of the university seal. Until the stairwell's completion, there was no primary staircase in the six-story building whose main entrance was on the fourth level. This and other inconveniences during the project were well received by staff and patrons; there was a significant drop in sales, but not beyond what was expected.

UNIVERSITY OF NEW MEXICO
NEW MEXICO STUDENT UNION
ALBUQUERQUE, N.M.

SUBMITTED BY: Misty P. Salaz, Marketing Representative
FULL-TIME EQUIVALENT ENROLLMENT: 24,705
FOUR-YEAR, PUBLIC INSTITUTION
OPENED: 1959
REOPENED: June 2003
AREA RENOVATED: 157,000 sq. ft.
AREA ADDED: 15,000 sq. ft.
TOTAL AREA: 172,000 sq. ft.
ASSIGNABLE AREA: 64.4%
COST OF PROJECT: $25 million
SOURCE OF FUNDING: 99% student fees; 1% private donations
ARCHITECTS: Van Gilbert – Albuquerque, N.M.; WTW Architects – Pittsburgh, Pa.
FACILITIES ADDED: Three large meeting rooms, five medium-sized meeting rooms, eight small meeting rooms, 70 office spaces, a fast food venue, a multi-purpose lounge, a quiet/reading lounge, and seven video/pinball game terminals

The New Mexico Student Union was originally designed for 7,000 students, and its infrastructure and technology had become inadequate in serving the University of New Mexico population of almost 25,000 students. Before construction began, two years worth of research was conducted including site visits to states surrounding New Mexico. Students were involved in the process from start to finish, including members of the Student Union Building Board and Student Government. These students were able to survey undergraduate and graduate students to see what they wanted in their new Student Union building.

Since opening, the union has created a true community for students, with its Southwestern feel and look that is characteristic of New Mexico. It offers students a warm, friendly atmosphere along with technological capabilities needed for the 21st century such as wireless networking in the entire building, on-site audio-visual capabilities, interactive video conferencing, and 367 laptop ports with a satellite option.

SOUTHERN ILLINOIS UNIVERSITY–EDWARDSVILLE

MORRIS UNIVERSITY CENTER
EDWARDSVILLE, ILL.

SUBMITTED BY: Mary E. Robinson, Director
FULL-TIME EQUIVALENT ENROLLMENT: 13,500
FOUR-YEAR, PUBLIC INSTITUTION
OPENED: 1967
REOPENED: October 2003
TOTAL AREA: 200,000 sq. ft.
ASSIGNABLE SPACE: 75%
COST OF PROJECT: $19.3 million
SOURCE OF FUNDING: 99% student fees; 1% institution
ARCHITECT: Woolpert LLP – Fairview Heights, Ill.
FACILITIES ADDED OR EXPANDED: A bookstore, a dining room area, a medium-sized meeting room, a quiet/reading lounge, an information center, and a computer lab

Students were involved in the Morris University Center project from the beginning, serving on committees and providing feedback about campus life needs on campus. The improvements to the union have been significant in enhancing its appearance and expanding the services it offers. The campus now boasts the second full-service Starbucks cyberlounge on a college campus in the United States and the second Auntie Anne's Pretzel shop in the country [as of 2004].

Over the new construction for the kitchen, an outdoor events space that seats more than 100 was created. Inside, the dining room space was almost doubled. Minor improvements to the bookstore included building two display windows at the entrance and creating a large interior display window that looks out to the main level student lounge.

UNIVERSITY OF MANITOBA

STUDENTS' UNION UNIVERSITY CENTRE
WINNIPEG, MANITOBA

SUBMITTED BY: Steven D. Gaetz, Executive Director
FULL-TIME EQUIVALENT ENROLLMENT: 22,000
FOUR-YEAR, PUBLIC, URBAN INSTITUTION
OPENED: January 1970
REOPENED: September 2003
TOTAL AREA: 3,500 sq. ft.
AREA ADDED: 2,200 sq. ft.
ASSIGNABLE SPACE: 100%
COST OF PROJECT: $400,000 (U.S.)
SOURCE OF FUNDING: 100% student fees
ARCHITECT: GBR Architects – Winnipeg, Manitoba
FACILITIES EXPANDED: A quiet/reading lounge, a television lounge, eight e-mail stations, and a billiards room

The expansion of the Students' Union University Centre was a stunning visual display of students' ability to determine need, seek out the necessary resources and professional services required, and oversee such projects to meet the organizational motto of "Students Helping Students." Students at the institution hired the architect, designed the project, oversaw the construction, and paid for the project upon completion. Televisions, a new sound system, eight new computers (donated by Hewlett-Packard) with free Internet access, and comfortable new furnishings were added, resulting in spaces where students can relax, study, and have fun.

COLORADO STATE UNIVERSITY

LORY STUDENT CENTER
FT. COLLINS, COLO.

SUBMITTED BY: Karen McCormick, Coordinator, Budgets and Special Projects
FULL-TIME EQUIVALENT ENROLLMENT: 24,700
FOUR-YEAR, PUBLIC, URBAN INSTITUTION
OPENED: March 1962
REOPENED: November 2003
TOTAL AREA RENOVATED: 27,037 sq. ft.
ASSIGNABLE SPACE: 74.73%
COST OF PROJECT: $2.4 million
SOURCE OF FUNDING: 100% auxiliary bond refunding
ARCHITECT: OZ Architecture – Denver
FACILITY EXPANDED OR ADDED: Food court and four e-mail stations

This food court renovation began through student identification of desired improvements in the surroundings, food variety, and check-out procedures. A new flexible meal plan had made it possible for residence hall students to spend convenience dollars in the food court. This upswing in customer base strained the seating capacity and checkout stands. Food offerings were limited, and inefficient and labor-intensive food preparation practices challenged the staff.

Through a food service system audit and business plan proposal, it was recommended that some unprofitable in-house food venues be replaced by brand-name franchises. This hybrid model better positions the food court to respond to customer demands and market trends.

Student groups helped garner support for the project during its bond refunding and approval processes. Upon completion, the space featured expanded seating arranged in "neighborhoods" that promote an intimate-space feeling in a large open environment. Neighborhoods are defined by different seating types (tables and chairs, booths, stools, etc.), carpet patterns, and lighting.

Photos courtesy of Smith College

SMITH COLLEGE

SMITH COLLEGE CAMPUS CENTER
NORTHAMPTON, MASS.

SUBMITTED BY: Dawn Mays-Floyd, Director
FULL-TIME EQUIVALENT ENROLLMENT: 2,500
FOUR-YEAR, PRIVATE INSTITUTION
OPENED: August 2003
TOTAL AREA: 56,000 sq. ft.
PERCENT OF ASSIGNABLE SPACE: 59%
COST OF PROJECT: $17.3 million
SOURCE OF FUNDING: 90% private donations; 10% institution
ARCHITECT: Weiss/Manfredi Architects – New York City
FACILITIES ADDED OR EXPANDED: A multipurpose room, two large meeting rooms, a medium-sized meeting room, two small meeting rooms, a food service area, a bookstore, a quiet/reading lounge, a television lounge, an information center, eight e-mail stations, two billiards tables, three office spaces, a coffee house, locker area/check room, four multipurpose lounges, an outdoor plaza/patio, and an art gallery

Smith College prides itself on student governance and student involvement in most major college decisions. Students were members of the various committees that recommended the building of the Smith College Campus Center and also participated on the project planning committees.

The new Campus Center has a distinct design that members of the campus feel reflects the uniqueness of a women's college and transforms the campus into a vibrant, unified community. It includes a sweeping skylight that runs the length of the facility. In addition to providing wonderful natural light, the skylight outlines the curves and openness of the overall design. And the transparency of the glass walls and doors creates a welcoming environment not often found in buildings with dark walls and lengthy hallways.

45

2005

Georgia Institute of Technology

The University of Alabama

St. Cloud State University

Arizona State University–East

Tulsa Community College–Southeast

University of Toronto

Allegheny College

Purdue University

Wartburg College

University of Dayton

Virginia Commonwealth University

University of North Dakota

Renovation &

CONSTRUCTION
SHOWCASE

A trend in college union facilities in 2005 was a focus on flexible design. Multipurpose rooms that could be divided via air walls to serve as several meeting breakout rooms or one large ballroom were common. Additionally, with upgrading the "look" of the facilities, attention was given to making them functional in an ever-more technological environment. Wireless access was a "must" among many projects, and most included other "behind the scenes" upgrades that should last well into the future. And components were not isolated in separate wings; rather they were visually integrated. For instance, in many cases food preparation is now done in front of customers instead of in a back kitchen, student organization space includes window walls or balconies overlooking a gathering area, and in one case, the campus radio station now broadcasts from a central lobby area in the union.

GEORGIA INSTITUTE OF TECHNOLOGY

PENNY & ROE STAMPS STUDENT CENTER COMMONS
ATLANTA, GA.

SUBMITTED BY: Rich Steele, Director, Student Center
FULL-TIME EQUIVALENT ENROLLMENT: 16,841
FOUR-YEAR, PUBLIC, URBAN INSTITUTION
OPENED: August 1970
REOPENED: August 2004
TOTAL GROSS AREA: 161,176 sq.ft.
AREA RENOVATED: 49,000 sq. ft.
ASSIGNABLE AREA: 68%
COST OF PROJECT: $6.5 million
SOURCE OF FUNDING: 72% auxiliary services reserve funds; 23% private donations; 5% institution
ARCHITECT: Lyman Davison Dooley – Atlanta; WTW Architects – Pittsburg
FACILITIES ADDED OR EXPANDED: Two large meeting rooms, four small meeting rooms, a pub, a reading lounge, a television lounge, two e-mail stations, two office spaces, a food service area, a coffee house, a copy center, a hair salon, an information credenza, a travel agency, a convenience store, and an optical shop

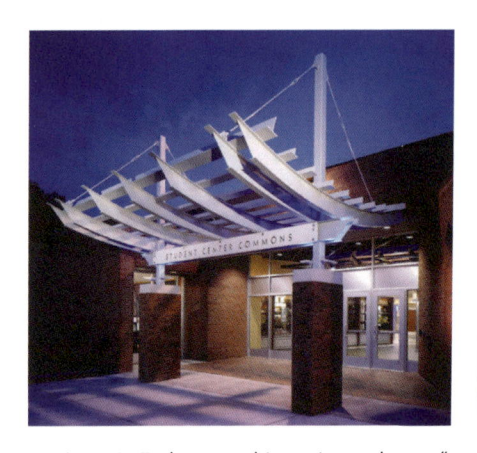

Georgia Tech wanted its union to be an "anchor destination" that would provide the "social glue" for the campus community. The project was highly successful. It produced a well-defined needs assessment at the inception, translated those needs into an effective schematic design, implemented the design through multiple construction delivery methods, and stayed close to original budget estimates through the entire three-year process. Students played a key role from the initial assessment stages through the grand opening celebration planning, chaired by students. The steering committee through the design and construction phase was one-third students as well.

The results have astounded the campus as all six of the primary functional needs were met and exceeded. Those functional requirements were: meeting space, organization space, gathering/study space, food service, performance/entertainment space, and service areas. The project unified four distinct facilities into one, utilizing the concept of "a river runs through it" to create significant traffic flow and vibrant areas. A central performance stage is topped with a skylight and surrounded by retail and lounge spaces. An open balcony was created on the second level to better relate student organization spaces with the active, heavily trafficked first level. Additionally, the facility now features an Irish-style pub (without alcohol). And, though challenging because of the need to install rooftop satellites and antenna and take extreme soundproofing measures, the campus radio station was relocated to the union and now jointly operates the performance stage.

THE UNIVERSITY OF ALABAMA
FERGUSON CENTER STUDENT UNION
TUSCALOOSA, ALA.

SUBMITTED BY: Kelli Knox-Hall, Assistant Director, Administrative Services and Development
FULL-TIME EQUIVALENT ENROLLMENT: 20,333
FOUR-YEAR, PUBLIC INSTITUTION
OPENED: 1972
REOPENED: January 2004
TOTAL GROSS AREA: 226,000 sq. ft.
AREA ADDED: 17,717 sq. ft.
ASSIGNABLE AREA: 85%
COST OF PROJECT: $7 million
SOURCE OF FUNDING: 67% institution, 33% food service contractor
ARCHITECT: KPS Group – Atlanta
FACILITIES ADDED OR EXPANDED: Two private dining rooms, a food service area, a ballroom, and two restrooms

Photos courtesy of Kelli Knox-Hall

The Ferguson Center Student Union's ballroom features all new flooring, fixtures, and lighting and is equipped with wireless Internet access. A new sound system complements the new facility along with a new, portable stage system.

The addition of the new food service area and the ballroom addition have not been without their challenges, including rainy weather that delayed the project by more than two months.

Overall reaction to the new food service area thus far has been positive, and student organizations are especially anxious to see final result of the ballroom. It is going to accommodate events on a much larger scale than before including honor society inductions, class ring presentations, recognition banquets, and late-night social programming as a part of the Healthy Campus 2010 initiative. The capacity for the ballroom doubled in size with maximum seating for a conference set-up at 1,300. A new sound system complements the new facility along with a new, portable stage system.

ST. CLOUD STATE UNIVERSITY
ATWOOD MEMORIAL CENTER
ST. CLOUD, MINN.

SUBMITTED BY: Margaret Vos, Director, Atwood Memorial Center
FULL-TIME EQUIVALENT ENROLLMENT: 12,355
FOUR-YEAR, PUBLIC INSTITUTION
OPENED: 1967
REOPENED: August 2004
EXISTING AREA: 163,528 sq. ft.
AREA RENOVATED: 36,275 sq. ft.
AREA ADDED: 18,278 sq. ft.
TOTAL AREA: 181,806 sq. ft.
ASSIGNABLE AREA: 92%
COST OF PROJECT: $8.1 million
SOURCE OF FUNDING: 100% student fees
ARCHITECT: GLT Architects – St. Cloud, Minn.
FACILITIES ADDED OR EXPANDED: A dining area, storage space, a credit union, bank, a campus ID card office, a coffee shop, offices, a medium-sized meeting room, an information desk, a copy center, two new retail spaces, a convenience store, a cultural center, a lounge and resource center, a workroom, a computer lab, three small meeting rooms, three large meeting rooms, a ballroom, and an auditorium

The renovation of the Atwood Memorial Center at St. Cloud State University set out to link to the campus's newly renovated student services center and bookstore via a walkway, improve retail space placement, increase space for student activities, and include a cultural center. All dreams were implemented.

Students were involved throughout the process, and the renovations were entirely funded by student fees, a referendum for which was approved by 85 percent of those voting. Students made site visits to other campuses and helped with the construction process (including bids), construction design, and grand-opening celebration. The members of the planning committee remained constant throughout the process, which made decision making fast and easy.

In fact, the project was ahead of schedule, within budget, and met all needs. The facility also has the honor of being the first in Minnesota to use design-build in the construction process. Some unique features of the renovated facility include the "Common Threads" art design on terrazzo floor (design by Sears and Myklebust), foot bath, new retail spaces, cultural center, and larger student organization space including a room just for archived files. The entire project was done without any interruption to student/faculty/staff services. The doors not only stayed open, but also it continued to be a busy place—12,000 daily traffic.

ARIZONA STATE UNIVERSITY–EAST

ASU–EAST STUDENT UNION
MESA, ARIZ.

SUBMITTED BY: Mike Mader, Director, Student Activities/Student Union
FULL-TIME EQUIVALENT ENROLLMENT: 2,594
FOUR-YEAR, PUBLIC INSTITUTION
OPENED: August 2004
TOTAL GROSS AREA: 27,000 sq. ft.
AREA ADDED: 27,000 sq. ft.
ASSIGNABLE AREA: 83%
COST OF PROJECT: $5.4 million
SOURCE OF FUNDING: 83% state; 14% institution; 3% private donations
ARCHITECT: Gould Evans – Phoenix
FACILITIES ADDED OR EXPANDED: A television lounge, seven offices, a small meeting room, a bookstore, an information center, two computer labs, a tennis table, an air hockey table, a foosball game, a billiards table, a snack bar, a food service area, a coffee house, a locker/check room area, a ballroom, three outdoor patios, and a student organization resource room

Arizona State University–East was the former Williams Air Force Base, and its union was the former Officers' Club. Another facility, the old "mess hall," was serving as the campus dining hall. The campus was in need of new, modern facilities to meet basic dining and meeting room/conference needs. After Propostion 301 passed in 2000, ASU–East received $27.5 million for campus improvements; the new union project received approximately $4.6 million of that amount. A cross-functional team of students, faculty, and staff was put in place to plan the facility. Ideas and feedback were garnered through focus groups, site visits, and open forums.

To make the most of the modest budget, the team developed a design that allowed for overlapping functions and made generous use of exterior spaces to make the facility appear bigger than its 27,000 square feet. Expansive glass walls, carefully shaded to prevent direct sunlight from entering the building, and five operable "garage doors" invite students into the union. At night, the glass walls take on another look—the lighted interior becomes a welcoming beacon on campus. The building design was driven by its relationship to the surrounding environment, and was sited to act as an anchor for a future pedestrian mall and plaza space.

While dining, bookstore, and meeting space make up most of the facility's small footprint, it has made a huge impact on campus life. Many have said, "this place feels like a college campus now."

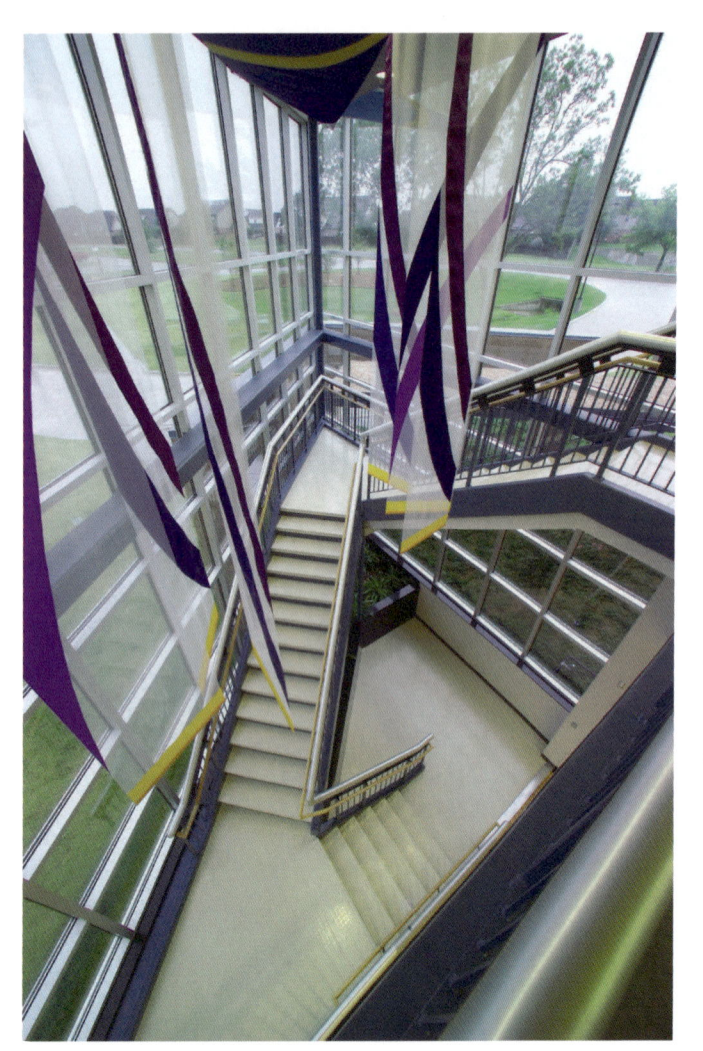

TULSA COMMUNITY COLLEGE–SOUTHEAST

STUDENT UNION
TULSA, OKLA.

Photos by Jon Petersen

SUBMITTED BY: Barbara Slagle, Director of Student Activities
FULL-TIME EQUIVALENT ENROLLMENT: 3,500
TWO-YEAR, PUBLIC, URBAN INSTITUTION
OPENED: January 2004
EXISTING AREA: 44,298 sq. ft.
AREA RENOVATED: 44,298 sq. ft.
AREA ADDED: 40,000 sq. ft.
TOTAL AREA: 84,298 sq. ft.
ASSIGNABLE AREA: 80%
COST OF PROJECT: $5.25 million
SOURCE OF FUNDING: 100% student fees
ARCHITECT: Dewberry – Tulsa, Okla.
FACILITIES ADDED OR EXPANDED: A multipurpose room, a large meeting room, two medium-sized meeting rooms, a small meeting room, a bookstore, an auditorium, a television lounge, a computer lounge, a cyber café, a ticket office, a fitness center, and an art gallery

The union at Tulsa Community College–Southeast was built in 1986—and looked it! The design was done without input from students, faculty, or staff. All the walls in the building were white, and no one was allowed to hang artwork. The furniture was boxy, heavy, and difficult to rearrange (which was necessary for most events). There was only one meeting room, inadequate storage, an activities/ticket office hidden on the lower level, and no fitness facilities.

In 2001, the campus began renovating the building and adding a fitness center. Foremost was the desire for input from all the facility's users. Students were surveyed about specific fitness equipment, positioning of the equipment, food service style, need for lounge space and meeting rooms, etc. During the rest of the process, students, faculty, and staff members participated in construction meetings, reviewed plans, and were involved in the opening ceremonies.

Changing how space was assigned allowed for a cyber café, coffee house space, four meeting rooms, additional storage, more display space in the bookstore, updates in the gallery including lighting and humidity controls, and a whole new look for the building. The new construction includes the fitness center, office space for the student activities and ticket office, a loading dock, and an easily identified entrance to the building (something missing previously, which had a negative impact on the facility's identity). Connecting the new construction to the old has allowed for a more legitimate image as a union rather than a student center, and the entire project has made it more appealing for campus community members, potential students, and visitors.

UNIVERSITY OF TORONTO

HART HOUSE
TORONTO, ONTARIO

Photos courtesy of Chris Lea

SUBMITTED BY: Chris Lea, Facility Manager
FULL-TIME EQUIVALENT ENROLLMENT: 44,200
URBAN, PUBLIC INSTITUTION
OPENED: November 1919
COMPLETED: September 2004
AREA RENOVATED: 1,500 sq. ft.
TOTAL AREA: 240,000 sq. ft.
ASSIGNABLE AREA: 47.4%
COST OF PROJECT: $1.6 million
SOURCE OF FUNDING: 34.5% self-financed; 25% government; 20% student fees; 15.5% institution; 5% other
ARCHITECT: Ihor Kotowycz, Capital Projects Division, University of Toronto – Toronto

Opened in 1919, Hart House is the most public building at the University of Toronto. However, because it is historically listed, just adding a light fixture can be a challenge, so constructing an elevator within it seems miraculous. Prior to this project, only 20 percent of the building was easily accessible and another 40 percent was accessible by taking people through back-of-house areas to freight elevators and what was basically a large dumbwaiter. The theater, located in the basement, was completely inaccessible to people in wheelchairs or scooters. After the renovation, about 80 percent of the building was easily accessible.

In the 1990s, students initiated the Students' Administrative Council Wheelchair Access Fund, which financed wheelchair accessibility to many campus buildings. The group donated $175,000 CDN to this fund (about $150,000 USD). An additional $210,000 CDN (about $176,000 USD) was raised for this project specifically through a student-led fee increase.

The construction was not without complications. Hart House is built over Taddle Creek, which was buried in the 19th century. Once in a while, especially after extended rain, Taddle Creek expresses itself, flooding parts of the sub-basement. For that reason, it was decided to use a holeless hydrolic elevator. (The last thing anyone wanted to deal with was a geyser in the elevator pit!) Another glitch was finding out the elevator pistons, which are long and weigh several tons, needed to be taken apart to fit into the pit. But after conquering these challenges, the elevator looks original to the building; the stonework and brass doors are especially beautiful.

ALLEGHENY COLLEGE

HENDERSON CAMPUS CENTER
MEADVILLE, PENN.

SUBMITTED BY: Ellen Kauffmann Nolan, Director of Student Activities
FULL-TIME EQUIVALENT ENROLLMENT: 1,950
FOUR-YEAR, PRIVATE INSTITUTION
OPENED: September 1970
REOPENED: Febuary 2004
EXISTING AREA: 71,616 sq. ft.
AREA RENOVATED: 48,960 sq. ft.
AREA ADDED: 12,400 sq. ft.
TOTAL AREA: 84,016 sq. ft.
ASSIGNABLE AREA: 75%
COST OF PROJECT: $8.6 million
SOURCE OF FUNDING: 100% private donations
ARCHITECT: William Brennan, Celli Flynn Brennan Turkel Associates – Pittsburgh, Pa.
FACILITIES ADDED OR EXPANDED: A large meeting room, a medium-sized meeting room, two small meeting rooms, a bookstore, an outdoor plaza/patio, three multipurpose lounges, an office space, a post office, two video/pinball machine areas, a billiards area, and an e-mail station

Photos by Bill Owen

While the Henderson Campus Center has a modern feel, elements of the nearly 200-year student experience at Allegheny College have been woven into the space. Memorabilia is housed in the food court, images of the mascot and campus logo are tiled into the floor in various locations, and new "lore" has been created for the campus history, such as the booths in the food court whose end pieces are "A's" for Allegheny. The campus radio station was moved from the third floor (where they stored records in a bathroom) to a highly visible first floor location with windows to the campus center lobby so deejays can be heard and seen. A staircase was removed to add 33 percent flexible space to the lobby, allowing for more performance space and flexible use. The food court underwent complete renovation; 80 percent of the food preparation happens in front of customers now.

Students were involved at every phase—from the preplanning to the finite details such as paint color and fabric choices. Through visits to residence halls and student organization meetings, students registered opinions, viewed plans, and contributed to planning. Students tested furniture, chose paint colors, and helped brainstorm design features such as the seal of the college in our lobby floor. Throughout the renovation roughly 400 of the 1,950 students toured the building to gauge progress, provide feedback, and generate excitement among their peers.

Photos courtesy of Terry Clayton

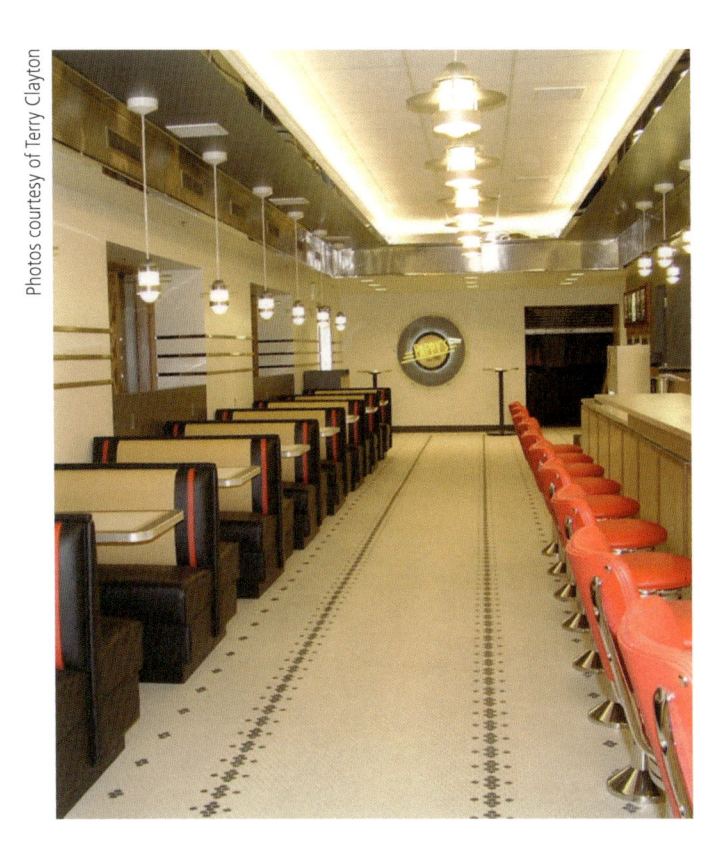

PURDUE UNIVERSITY

PURDUE MEMORIAL UNION
PAPPY'S – THE ORIGINAL SWEET SHOP
WEST LAFAYETTE, IND.

SUBMITTED BY: Terry Clayton, Assistant Director, Purdue Memorial Union
FULL-TIME EQUIVALENT ENROLLMENT: 38,900
FOUR-YEAR, PUBLIC, URBAN INSTITUTION
OPENED: September 1927
REOPENED: July 2004
AREA RENOVATED: 4,454 sq. ft.
TOTAL AREA: 4,454 sq. ft.
ASSIGNABLE AREA: 94%
COST OF PROJECT: $1.5 million
SOURCE OF FUNDING: 100% institution
ARCHITECT: Scholer Corporation – Lafayette, Ind.
FACILITY RENOVATED: A quick service venue

In 1927, Pappy's was the first dining facility built in the Purdue Memorial Union at Purdue University. Originally developed as a soda fountain counter, Pappy's restaurant had gone many years with little update. Pappy's looked tired, there were constant equipment repairs, revenue was declining each year, and most importantly there were many customer complaints. Staff soon decided to give Pappy's a major renovation and a new look and concept.

Students were involved in every aspect of the planning, and alumni took a vested interest from a nostalgic perspective. A "diner concept" did not exist on the Purdue campus, but it kept coming up in planning discussions. It was decided that primary goals of the project would be: a diner-like appearance, providing excitement, and maintaining the myth or lore of the historical sweet shop.

Pappy's now features stainless steel and polished chrome, tile floors, padded booths, refurbished jukeboxes, and neon signs. There is space to gather and more private seating for studying. The menu focuses heavily on burgers, shakes, and fries, although also served are student-requested salads and vegetarian offerings. Employees wear white shirts, black pants, black bowties, and paper hats as hair restraints. Perhaps the most noteworthy aspect to the project was the ability to move the engineered cooking area to allow greater visibility both from a guest's viewpoint as well as opening it up to the hallway. Counter seating, booths, and round tabletops surround this cooking area.

Upon completion, rave reviews came from alumni of all ages as well as from current students, staff, and faculty. As they say at Purdue, "Pappy's, Original in 1927 and Still Original Today."

WARTBURG COLLEGE

SAEMANN STUDENT CENTER
WAVERLY, IOWA

SUBMITTED BY: Matt B. Pries, Director of the Student Center
FULL-TIME EQUIVALENT ENROLLMENT: 1,761
FOUR-YEAR, PRIVATE INSTITUTION
REOPENED: September 2004
EXISTING AREA: 41,295 sq. ft.
AREA RENOVATED: 36,233 sq. ft.
AREA ADDED: 44,520 sq. ft.
TOTAL AREA: 83,355 sq. ft.
ASSIGNABLE AREA: 69.2%
COST OF PROJECT: $15 million
SOURCE OF FUNDING: 50% private donations; 43% institution; 7% student fees
ARCHITECT: WTW Architects – Pittsburgh, Pa.
FACILITIES ADDED OR EXPANDED: Three large meeting rooms, three small meeting rooms, a restaurant, a bookstore, a theater, five quiet/reading lounges, two television lounges, an information center, a post office and student mailboxes, four e-mail stations, 24 offices, two private dining rooms, another food service area, a ticket office, a copy center, wireless capability, and a student organization hub

After nine consecutive years of record enrollment and increased use of the facility by outside groups, Wartburg College needed to expand and renovate its union. In addition to the students, staff, faculty, and alumni who were on the Commission Wartburg task force, students from major organizations (e.g., Student Senate, Campus Programming) were involved in the planning for the renovation.

The Saemann Student Center now affords more opportunities for students to come together, and it accommodates outside groups more fully with conference and convention needs. Three large meeting rooms also function as ballrooms and can be used individually, in a set of two, or as one room seating up to 400 for banquets or up to 500 for theater-style seating. The second floor concourse is not only a main circulation space, but also a lounge and eating area, curving to provide a panoramic view of campus. There are 10 food service venues available in the cafeteria. All meeting rooms have built-in audio-visual capabilities. And a student organizational hub was designed to accommodate all recognized campus groups and provide office space for the six largest groups including a conference room.

The completed Saemann Student Center is a facility of which its campus is proud. The project incorporates an elevated pedestrian walkway system with connecting bridges and concourse to adjacent buildings. The materials and details used in the design blend well with other buildings, and its mass, scale, and character reflecting the unique German heritage of the college.

Photos courtesy of Wartburg College

UNIVERSITY OF DAYTON
THE HANGAR
DAYTON, OHIO

Photos courtesy of Amy Lopez

SUBMITTED BY: Amy D. Lopez, Director of Kennedy Union and Conference Services
FULL-TIME EQUIVALENT ENROLLMENT: 6,500
FOUR-YEAR, PRIVATE INSTITUTION
OPENED: 1964
REOPENED: August 2004
AREA RENOVATED: 10,071 sq. ft.
TOTAL AREA: 10,071 sq. ft.
ASSIGNABLE AREA: 100%
COST OF PROJECT: $1.25 million
SOURCE OF FUNDING: 80% private donations; 20% institution
ARCHITECT: Greg Martz, Edge & Tinney Architects – Dayton, Ohio
AMMENITIES ADDED OR EXPANDED: A television lounge, four new bowling lanes, a food service area, four e-mail stations, four video/pinball machines, six new billiards tables, a juke box, and an outdoor patio

The games room at the University of Dayton had become outdated. Its equipment was 40 years old, there was no natural lighting, and students were no longer spending time in the space. Two alumni decided to fund the renovation of the room, but wanted to do so with student input.

Students were involved in every phase of the project. Through an April 2003 EBI survey about the games room renovation, planners learned that students wanted more lounge space on campus. This became a key design element. An advisory group of students, faculty, and staff was assembled to provide input and decision making as the new games room concept was developed.

Much-needed lounge space was added to the games room so that students would hang out in the space rather than use it as a pass-through to somewhere else on campus. The hallway wall and external wall were replaced with glass to allow people to look into and out of the space, and to allow for more natural lighting in the room. As a result, the Hangar has become a heavily used recreation space and student hang-out.

VIRGINIA COMMONWEALTH UNIVERSITY
UNIVERSITY STUDENT COMMONS
RICHMOND, VA.

SUBMITTED BY: Kirsten Hirsch, Assistant Director for Public Relations
FULL-TIME EQUIVALENT ENROLLMENT: 28,462
FOUR-YEAR, PUBLIC, URBAN INSTITUTION
OPENED: April 2004
EXISTING AREA: 120,323 sq. ft.
AREA RENOVATED: 16,285 sq. ft.
AREA ADDED: 35,151 sq. ft.
TOTAL AREA: 171,759 sq. ft.
ASSIGNABLE AREA: 77%
COST OF PROJECT: $9.8 million
SOURCE OF FUNDING: 100% student fees
ARCHITECT: Clark Nexson – Norfolk, Va.
FACILITIES ADDED OR EXPANDED: A ballroom, a theater, two food courts, and multiple lounges

Photos courtesy of Kirsten Hirsch

The student population at Virginia Commonwealth University grew from 21,680 students in 1996 to 28,462 students in 2004. Additional meeting and event space was desperately needed to accommodate a growing student organization base, the demand for more student programming, and the university's interest in conference services. An online survey was conducted in 2000, which guided the design committee. Students served on the design and grand opening committees and were constantly apprised of developments through presentations to the Student Government Association, student advisory committees, and a dynamic and interactive website. A webcam was installed prior to groundbreaking to give the entire campus a consistent view of the construction process.

Because the university is located in an urban area, land is limited. There are four noteworthy features of the addition. A first-floor concourse was enclosed, adding needed interior square footage while still accommodating the major thoroughfare. On the second floor, the existing two ballrooms and a new third ballroom were connected by a series of lounges, enclosing a portion of the roof. The result is a conference planner's dream, with all three ballrooms, the newly renovated Commons Theater, and expansive lounges all accessible on one level. The existing food courts were renovated to create two separate service areas, one of which can also serve for late night dining. The last is the Grand Staircase overlooking an expanded and renovated outdoor plaza. Already, it has become a popular gathering place for the university community.

UNIVERSITY OF NORTH DAKOTA

UND MEMORIAL UNION
GRAND FORKS, N.D.

Photos courtesy of Cory Hilliard

SUBMITTED BY: Cory Hilliard, Assistant Director Business Services
FULL-TIME EQUIVALENT ENROLLMENT: 13,187
FOUR-YEAR, PUBLIC INSTITUTION
OPENED: May 1951
REOPENED: August 2004
AREA RENOVATED: 133,000 sq. ft.
TOTAL AREA: 133,000 sq. ft.
ASSIGNABLE AREA: 70%
COST OF PROJECT: $4.7 million
SOURCE OF FUNDING: 75% student fees; 25% institution
ARCHITECT: JLG Architects – Minneapolis and Grand Forks, N.D.
FACILITIES ADDED OR EXPANDED: A multipurpose room, two large meeting rooms, nine medium-sized meeting rooms, a convenience store, a food court, a crafts center, an auditorium, four television lounges, an information center, a computer lab, eight e-mail stations, a table tennis table, 10 billiards tables, an outdoor equipment center, nine office spaces, a coffee house, a locker/check room, a photo dark room, a box office, a ballroom, a multipurpose lounge, and a copy center

The need to renovate the University of North Dakota Memorial Union was obvious after a flood devastated much of the university and union in 1997. Additionally, in 2000, the bookstore departed for a new location north of campus, creating a huge void on the main level. A renovation committee was formed with staff and students, and surveys were conducted to assess the campus's needs for the union. Students were included in every aspect; they held positions on each committee and subcommittee formed to select everything from paint and carpet colors to naming of programming areas.

What resulted was the largest renovation project the union had seen since its initial construction in 1951. Through it all, every service offered in the union before the project began was still available to the campus community in some shape or form during and after the renovation. From office space to multipurpose rooms to an expansive food court, the campus enjoys the completed facility, especially its most noticeable addition and main-level focal point, a glass wall with current and historical images from the university's rich history and culture that represent the school's "Tradition," "Pride," and "Community."

2006

University of Minnesota–Crookston

Minnesota State University–Mankato

Creighton University

Appalachian State University

University of Maryland–College Park

University of Missouri–Rolla

University of Utah

College of Charleston

Wichita State University

Youngstown State University

RENOVATION + CONSTRUCTION
showcase

This 2006 Renovation and Construction Showcase features a range of impressive union projects completed in 2005. From a new college union pharmacy to a completely new college union, each of the 11 projects featured on the following pages has a unique story. We also modified the submission form this year to distinguish between expanded and added features. Also new this year was a question about wireless access and separate data fields for different kinds of dining operations. All this is meant to assist other unions in determining trends in union building projects.

Photo by David Harvey and courtesy of MHTN

Minnesota State University–Mankato, Centennial Student Union

UNIVERSITY OF MINNESOTA–CROOKSTON
Student Center (new building)
Crookston, Minn.

SUBMITTED BY: Pamela Holsinger-Fuchs, Vice Chancellor for Student Services
FULL-TIME EQUIVALENT ENROLLMENT: 1,200
FOUR-YEAR, PUBLIC, RURAL
OPENED: June 2005
TOTAL GROSS AREA: 38,500 sq. ft.
AREA RENOVATED: 1,500 sq. ft.
AREA ADDED: 37,000 sq. ft.
ASSIGNABLE AREA: 70%
PROJECT COST: $6 million plus other project costs
FUNDING SOURCE: 100% state government
ARCHITECT: Mark Lundberg – Moorhead, Minn.
FACILITIES ADDED: A bookstore, five multipurpose rooms, an information center, 18 offices, two meeting rooms, and wireless Internet access

Photos courtesy of Pamela Holsinger-Fuchs

In many ways, the new union at the University of Minnesota–Crookston is a vast departure from its predecessor. The earlier building, built in the 1930s, suffered from mold in its walls and bad wiring during recent years. The new facility, which opened in June 2005, boasts modern features like a commuter-student lounge, coffee house, and television and music lounges. Other amenities include storage for student organizations and a reading room. But parts of the 1930s-era building live on. Pieces of it, like its fireplace mantle, light fixtures, even some of its bricks, were salvaged and incorporated into the new facility.

Another important component of this project was student involvement, said Pamela Holsinger-Fuchs, vice chancellor for student services. "Students were involved in every aspect of the process," from planning to building, she said. "The contractor was the father of our student body president, so [the daughter] ended up working on the project as a laborer."

MINNESOTA STATE UNIVERSITY–MANKATO
Centennial Student Union (renovation)
Mankato, Minn.

The Centennial Student Union needed a facelift and some mandatory upkeep work. Its south face had an "undistinguished appearance," said Michael Hodapp, interim union director, and lacked an adequate entry. In addition, $3 million in deferred maintenance issues were identified.

Several processes were used to determine what would be supported. The union board and student association participated in planning sessions, studies, and focus groups. Planners held open forums with students in the union lounge, asking for feedback on different proposals.

The result was a project that addressed both maintenance and cosmetic issues, and "transformed [the union] from a basic utilitarian facility to the showplace of the campus," Hodapp said. "The building is both dramatic and highly useable," and includes a three-story Hearth Lounge. Students seem to agree; since the renovation, building counts and dining sales have increased more than 40 percent.

SUBMITTED BY: Michael Hodapp, Interim Director, Centennial Student Union
FULL-TIME EQUIVALENT ENROLLMENT: 14,000
FOUR-YEAR, PUBLIC
REOPENED: March 2005
TOTAL GROSS AREA: 206,577 sq. ft.
AREA RENOVATED: 60,000 sq. ft.
AREA ADDED: 10,000 sq. ft.
ASSIGNABLE AREA: 53%
PROJECT COST: $12 million
FUNDING SOURCE: 100% student fees
ARCHITECT: Paulsen Architects/MHTN – Mankato, Minn. and Salt Lake City
FACILITIES ADDED: A multipurpose room, a snack bar, a private room, an information center, office space, an art gallery, and a bank
FACILITIES RENOVATED: Four meeting rooms, six branded food venues, two cafeterias, a computer lab, and wireless access

Photos by David Harvey and courtesy of MHTN

Photos courtesy of Rowland W. Hughes

SUBMITTED BY: Rowland W. Hughes, Director of Skutt Student Center
FULL-TIME EQUIVALENT ENROLLMENT: 6,408
FOUR-YEAR, PRIVATE, URBAN
OPENED: September 1987
REOPENED: August 2005
TOTAL GROSS AREA: 56,000 sq. ft.
AREA RENOVATED: 8,892 sq. ft.
ASSIGNABLE AREA: 88%
PROJECT COST: $1.3 million
FUNDING SOURCE: 32% institution; 62% vendor investment
ARCHITECT: Sinclair/Hille Architects – Lincoln, Neb.
FACILITIES RENOVATED: Three branded food venues, a snack bar, a reading lounge, a television lounge, a games room, one computer lab, three offices, a food court, a coffee house, one area with wireless access, and an art gallery

CREIGHTON UNIVERSITY
Skutt Student Center (renovation)
Omaha, Neb.

For its 18th birthday, the Skutt Student Center received a major makeover. Although the facility was ahead of its time in 1987, "food service venues and technology trends over the years had outpaced it," said Rowland W. Hughes, the union's director. To catch up, a $1.3 million renovation was undertaken. The project included the addition of 68 seats for food service, a beverage bar, and an upscale food court supplied by branded venues and University Dining Services. To expand late-night programming options, a six-station gaming area, three viewing screens, and a large screen plasma television were installed, as were wireless access and hardwired ports for laptops. The new lighting system maximizes space by focusing on previously unused areas and can be adjusted for different events. Spotlights make future art exhibits a possibility. Architectural details salvaged from an older campus building were incorporated into the renovation, "creating a historical link for alumni," Hughes said. In terms of the current student body, "the project has re-energized the college union."

APPALACHIAN STATE UNIVERSITY
Plemmons Student Union (renovation)
Boone, N.C.

As unions become increasingly wired, Appalachian State University's new addition is a different kind of hot spot. The Plemmons Student Union Solarium "gets high traffic from students, faculty, and staff, proving that this dynamic area is definitely a new hot spot on campus," said Dave Robertson, director of student programs. The Solarium houses four waterfalls and an abundance of indoor trees and plant life. The space can be used for informal studying and socializing, as well as reserved for special events, and it has become a highlight of campus tours, Robertson said.

SUBMITTED BY: Dave Robertson, Director of Student Programs
FULL-TIME EQUIVALENT ENROLLMENT: 13,500
FOUR-YEAR, PUBLIC, RURAL
REOPENED: January 2005
TOTAL GROSS AREA: 130,000 sq. ft.
AREA ADDED: 15,000 sq. ft.
ASSIGNABLE AREA: 90%
PROJECT COST: $3 million
FUNDING SOURCE: 100% student fees
ARCHITECT: Perkins+Will –Charlotte, N.C.
FACILITIES ADDED: A multipurpose room and wireless access

Photos courtesy of Dave Robertson

UNIVERSITY OF MARYLAND—COLLEGE PARK
Adele H. Stamp Student Union (renovation)
College Park, Md.

SUBMITTED BY: Stephen K. Gnadt, Associate Director of Student Union
FULL-TIME EQUIVALENT ENROLLMENT: 34,000
FOUR-YEAR, PUBLIC, URBAN
REOPENED: April 2005
TOTAL GROSS AREA: 286,092 sq. ft.
AREA RENOVATED: 256,054 sq. ft.
AREA ADDED: 30,038 sq. ft.
ASSIGNABLE AREA: 60%
PROJECT COST: $57.5 million
FUNDING SOURCE: 60% student fees; 40% union-generated revenue
ARCHITECT: Sasaki Associates/CHK Joint Venture – Watertown, Mass.
FACILITIES ADDED: A multipurpose room, two large meeting rooms, five small meeting rooms, seven branded food venues, a reading lounge, a television lounge, two offices, 45 student organization offices, and wireless access
FACILITIES EXPANDED: Two multipurpose rooms, three large meeting rooms, two branded food venues, a bookstore, a crafts center, a theater, an information center, eight bowling lanes, a games room, 10 offices, a coffee house, a locker room, a photography room, three student organization offices, a box office, two ballrooms, an art gallery, an outdoor patio, a copy center, and a full service bank

The University of Maryland–College Park has successfully brought its college union into the 21st century. It took 14 years—eight for planning, six for construction—but that's the reality of undertaking a major renovation project while keeping a union's doors open.

Stephen K. Gnadt, associate director of the Adele H. Stamp Student Union, believes other schools contemplating a phased renovation project might prepare by learning about University of Maryland's project. The process began in the late 1980s, when the Union Into the 21st Century Task Force gathered to assess the union and its role on campus. It concluded that, in addition to minor maintenance issues, the facility had a disorienting functional arrangement, fragmented layout, and lack of appropriate signage. Overall, it was deemed inadequate and inconsistent with the stature of the campus and its importance. A plan addressing these issues was approved in 1995.

Construction began in 1997, and was executed in four phases. "Portions of the building were closed down, programs and services were relocated ... and then new functions moved into their new spaces," Gnadt said. During the height of construction, union traffic averaged 17,000 people per day. Since reopening, that number has increased to 23,000.

Photos courtesy of Stephen K. Gnadt

Photos courtesy of Mark Potrafka

UNIVERSITY OF MISSOURI–ROLLA
Havener Center (new building)
Rolla, Mo.

Rather than renovate pre-existing buildings, the University of Missouri decided to build a new union to meet its campus' needs. The institution needed "larger, more flexible spaces than what the previous buildings offered," said Mark Potrafka, director of student life. "The students approved the creation of a master plan and later approved $12.5 million for a new center."

The Havener Center offers wireless access, keyless entry, lounge space, as well as multiple meeting rooms that can be reconfigured based on programming needs. Since opening, patronage is 40 percent higher than at the previous union buildings, and auxiliary income has nearly doubled.

SUBMITTED BY: Mark Potrafka, Director of Student Life
FULL-TIME EQUIVALENT ENROLLMENT: 5,100
FOUR-YEAR, PUBLIC
OPENED: January 2005
TOTAL GROSS AREA: 105,000 sq. ft.
ASSIGNABLE AREA: 57%
PROJECT COST: $17.5 million
FUNDING SOURCE: 70% student fees; 30% private funding
ARCHITECT: Dickinson Hussman Architects – St. Louis
FACILITIES ADDED: Ten meeting rooms, nine branded food venues, a cafeteria, a bookstore, a reading lounge, a television lounge, an information center, two computer labs, games room, 10 offices, a student organization storage area, six student organization offices, a ballroom, an outdoor patio, wireless access, two art galleries, a poster service, 12 student group work spaces, a bank, and a board room

SUBMITTED BY: Whit Hollis, Director
FULL-TIME EQUIVALENT ENROLLMENT: 24,000
PUBLIC, FOUR-YEAR, URBAN
OPENED: 1957
REOPENED: January 2005
TOTAL GROSS AREA: 206,000 sq. ft.
AREA RENOVATED: 10,161 sq. ft.
ASSIGNABLE AREA: 6.3%
PROJECT COST: $500,000
FUNDING SOURCE: 100% student fees
ARCHITECT: Gould Evans Associates – Salt Lake City
FACILITIES ADDED: Pharmacy
FACILITIES EXPANDED: A television lounge, an information center, a computer lab, a games room, and bowling lanes

UNIVERSITY OF UTAH
A. Ray Olpin University Union (renovation)
Salt Lake City

The A. Ray Olpin University Union at the University of Utah, built in the late 1950s, is a case study of what can happen without a plan. As the university had grown during the last 50 years, "new programs and offices … had a tendency to be placed in the union," said Whit Hollis, director. Lacking a master plan, offices were arranged haphazardly and space used injudiciously. Spaces that "could generate income for the building operation were instead used for offices," he added.

This renovation involved opening several small pre-existing spaces into one larger space. The area now includes bowling lanes, a television lounge, vending, and a gaming area. In addition, the school's first unisex restroom was built as was a pharmacy. Facility traffic has increased, meaning more students and faculty are being exposed to the union's programs. "This is an example of how smaller projects can have a significant impact on facilities and services," Hollis said. "Not everyone can afford building a new union."

UNIVERSITY OF UTAH
A. Ray Olpin University Union (renovation)
Salt Lake City

AREA RENOVATED: 4,345 sq. ft.
ASSIGNABLE AREA: 4.57%
PROJECT COST: $140,000
FUNDING SOURCE: 100% student fees
ARCHITECT: Gould Evans Associates – Salt Lake City
FACILITIES EXPANDED: A faculty/staff dining area

It didn't take much to improve the look and feel of the faculty/staff dining area at the A. Ray Olpin University Union. The eating area was last renovated in the early 1970s, Hollis said, and as a result, "the look and feel of the space was dark and uninviting even with an outstanding view of the Great Salt Lake, the Salt Lake Valley, and surrounding mountains." To achieve a modern, welcoming look, older features were removed and newer ones installed. "This renovation did not add space or alter dimensions," Hollis said. "It just opened it up, made the space brighter by removing window tinting and curtains, and adding modern lighting and fixtures." The $140,000 project was funded entirely through student fees, and was one of two renovations at the union in 2005.

SUBMITTED BY: Susan H. Payment, Director of Student Life
FULL-TIME EQUIVALENT ENROLLMENT: 11,607
FOUR-YEAR, PUBLIC, URBAN
OPENED: 1974
REOPENED: August 2005
TOTAL GROSS AREA: 57,000 sq. ft.
AREA RENOVATED: 57,000 sq. ft
ASSIGNABLE AREA: 70%
PROJECT COST: $6.1 million
FUNDING SOURCE: 100% institution
ARCHITECT: LS3P – Charleston, S.C.
FACILITIES EXPANDED: Seven meeting rooms, an information center, a computer lab, 13 offices, two student organization offices, a games room, a fitness equipment room, a ballroom, an oudoor patio, wireless access, a poster service, and a copy center

COLLEGE OF CHARLESTON
Theodore S. Stern Student Center (renovation)
Charleston, S.C.

"If you renovate it, they will come," is Susan H. Payment's new slogan. Director of student life at the College of Charleston, Payment is amazed at how quickly and enthusiastically the campus community has embraced the newly renovated college union. In the four months since it reopened, "student groups can be found throughout the building, holding meetings, staging programs, and seeking out services," she said.

The union's newfound popularity proves that a "much-loved and well-used facility," once considered for demolition, can be reinvigorated through a well-planned renovation. The $6.1 million project, funded entirely by the institution, improved many of the original building's flaws, like dead-end hallways and dark corners. It also altered the ground level breezeway to include an information desk and lobby, two ATM machines, and an e-mail kiosk. The fitness center was expanded, and a three-story glass atrium was added, "providing light and a sense of community to the building that it had been lacking in the past," Payment said.

WICHITA STATE UNIVERSITY
Rhatigan Student Center (renovation)
Wichita, Kan.

It's easy to measure how much students like the new look and feel of the Rhatigan Student Center at Wichita State University. Since it reopened after a renovation in January 2005, students and organizations have reserved the college union's meeting space twice as much as they did before. Now, the Student Activities Council offers an average of four events per week in the renovated lounge area, Shocker Square.

Changes made to the lounge included taming the vibrant color scheme, which consisted of blue and orange furniture and red brick walls. "Painted sheetrock, wallpaper, wood laminate walls, bright carpet, and vinyl floor tiles with a wood-flooring look now bring in natural colors and stains complementary to the WSU sunflower yellow and black colors," said Jacob Brumfield, development manager. A glass door was installed to prevent lounge noise from seeping into other parts of the college union and vice versa.

Other significant changes were made to the college union's eating area, the Copperfields Dining Area. Student surveys indicated that the campus population wanted a branded food concept with familiar food products available. In addition, the dining area's layout was reconfigured. The original cafeteria style format was changed to one more suited to current students' "grab and go" dining habits.

SUBMITTED BY: Jacob Brumfield, Development Manager
FULL-TIME EQUIVALENT ENROLLMENT: 10,370
FOUR-YEAR, PUBLIC, URBAN
REOPENED: January, 2005
TOTAL GROSS AREA: 177,146 sq. ft.
AREA RENOVATED: 3,700 sq. ft.
ASSIGNABLE AREA: 54.73%
PROJECT COST: $1 million
FUNDING SOURCES: 67% institution; 33% Sodexho Dining Services, student government, and Commerce Bank
ARCHITECT: Tod Ford, McCluggage, Van Sickle and Perry – Wichita, Kan.
FACILITIES ADDED: A branded food concept, a computer lab, and a dining area

Photos courtesy of Jack Fahey

YOUNGSTOWN STATE UNIVERSITY
Bookstore (renovated)
Youngstown, Ohio

SUBMITTED BY: Jack Fahey, Director of Auxiliary Services
FULL-TIME EQUIVALENT ENROLLMENT: 10,500
FOUR-YEAR, PUBLIC, URBAN
REOPENED: August 2005
TOTAL GROSS AREA: 20,000 sq. ft.
AREA ADDED: 4,000 sq. ft.
AREA RENOVATED: 16,000 sq. ft
ASSIGNABLE AREA: 92%
PROJECT COST: $1.6 million
FUNDING SOURCE: 100% bookstore
ARCHITECT: Strollo Architects/Michael Lopez Designs – Youngstown, Ohio, and Detroit

In addition to being the place to buy books and sundries, the renovated bookstore at Youngstown State University was slated to become a walkway between the college union and the new wellness center. When planning for the store's renovation, its first in 15 years, architects had to take into account its expanded function. They had to "overcome limitations imposed by a planned 12-foot-wide corridor through the center of the store," said Jack Fahey, director of auxiliary services, while also taking advantage of the addition. Architects focused on attracting traffic from both sides of the walkway. They installed department store showcase windows in the store's entrance for a modern look, and built a convenience store carrying items needed by students exercising in the wellness center. In all, 4,000 square feet were added, and students' requests for an "exciting shopping environment" that reflected the university's heritage were fulfilled.

2007

Christopher Newport University

Jacksonville University

University of Connecticut

California State University–Northridge

Colorado State University

Genesee Community College

Minnesota State University–Mankato

Philadelphia University

Phillips Exeter Academy

San Juan College

Southern Connecticut State University

Texas Tech University

University of North Carolina–Wilmington

Virginia Polytechnic Institute and State University

Eastern Michigan University

2007 RENOVATION and

Philadelphia University
Kanbar Campus Center
Philadelphia

Colorado State University
Lory Student Center
Transit Center

CONSTRUCTION SHOWCASE

In 2006, campuses from each coast and peppered throughout the continental United States completed renovation and construction projects. Some college unions were brand-new facilities many years in the making. Others were phased renovations or infrastructure upgrades, while still others renewed spaces through budget-friendly interior design. Regardless, they fit their respective campus's needs, and the outcomes are some grand student-centered facilities positioned to build campus community now and in the years to come. By sharing these projects, institutions considering a college union renovation or construction can learn more about the various approaches, complexities, and features of the buildings included in the following showcase.

Photos courtesy of Shaun McCready

Christopher Newport University
David Student Union (new building)
Newport News, Va.

Since the majority of the student population at Christopher Newport University was nonresidential, the original college union provided services for only 300 residential students. However, this has changed. Now, with 3,000 residential students [as of 2007], the university took on a project to construct a facility that would meet the needs of the new student population.

"The David Student Union brings together those services and students in a 'one-stop shop' in the heart of campus," said Shaun McCready, operations manager.

The new union provides space for more student organizations to have offices, many study and computing areas, along with an outdoor dining patio.

"The David Student Union's efficiency, style, beauty, and attention to detail perfectly complement its functionality," McCready said.

Submitted by: Shaun McCready, Operations Manager
Full-time equivalent enrollment: 4,793
Four-year, public
Opened: September 2006
Total gross area: 106,630 sq. ft.
Assignable Space: 77%
Project cost: $34.5 million
Architect: DMJM Architects and Engineers – Arlington, Va.
Facilities added: Formal and informal dining options, two-story bookstore, full-service post office, digital color copy center, grand ballroom, meeting and conference rooms, student organization offices, student newspaper offices, offices for career development, multicultural affairs, international studies, and academic advising, games and television rooms, study areas, computer terminals, and wireless Internet connection

Photos courtesy of Justin Camputaro

Jacksonville University
Davis Student Commons (renovation)
Jacksonville, Fla.

Before Davis Student Commons opened its doors on Oct. 10, 2006, Jacksonville University did not have a college union. "There was no main facility for student organizations to meet, no single location for students to hang out when not in class, no location for general recreation," said Justin Camputaro, director of campus activities and Davis Student Commons. "For the first time ever, all of the students have a place to hang out, hold organization meetings and events, and do so late at night."

Instead of constructing a completely new building, the university decided to renovate the old College of Business building into a union. Throughout the process, students provided the majority of the input for the Davis Student Commons.

"Since this building was to be dedicated to the students, they provided most of the direction for what was to be in the new building. Through the planning committee and regular surveys throughout the campus, the students were the architects," Camputaro said. "The resulting structure, which includes a unique all-glass expansion on the rear of the facility for the fitness center overlooking the St. John's River, is very unique from many other unions."

Submitted by: Justin Camputaro, Director of Campus Activities and Davis Student Commons
Full-time enrollment: 2,800
Four-year, private, urban
Reopened: October 2006
Area renovated: 35,867 sq. ft.
Area added: 2,254 sq. ft.
Assignable area: 75%
Project cost: $3.2 million
Funding source: 3% student fees; 81% private funding; 16% other
Architect: Reynolds, Smith and Hills, Inc. – Orlando
Facilities added: Three multipurpose rooms, one meeting room, two auditoriums, one faculty lounge, two quiet lounges, one television lounge, one information center, a computer lab, one games room, one food service area, one fitness room, and an outdoor patio
Facilities renovated: 13 office spaces and 11 student organization offices

Photos courtesy of Chuck Morrell

University of Connecticut
Student Union (renovation/addition)
Storrs, Conn.

The plans for renovating the college union at the University of Connecticut have been evolving since 1998. The process included input from student, faculty, staff, alumni, and even community members. And finally, in 2006, the project was completed.

"[The university is] very proud of the new Student Union," said Chuck Morrell, associate director of the Student Union. "The fact that the university and the state legislature funded the project completely speaks great volumes as to the commitment and support being provided to student affairs on our campus."

Morrell pointed out some of the features of the new building: "The 500-seat digital theater, Student Union ballroom, and several meeting rooms have been equipped with state-of-the-art media systems. The main area on the first floor has been named 'Union Street' and was designed to provide open lounge space in the center of high-traffic areas. The original building was maintained with the exterior facade left intact as part of the interior of the new facility," he said.

Submitted by: Chuck Morrell, Associate Director, Student Union
Full-time enrollment: 26,500
Four-year, public
Reopened: June 2006
Area renovated: 55,000 sq. ft.
Area added: 165,000 sq. ft.
Assignable area: 70.5%
Project cost: $70 million
Funding source: 100% UCONN2000 Fund
Architect: Cannon Design – Boston
Facilities added: Two multipurpose rooms, six large meeting rooms, eight medium-sized meeting rooms, two small reading rooms, three branded food concepts, one theater, two quiet lounges, one television lounge, one information center, one computer lab, a games room, one outdoor equipment room, nine office spaces, one food court, a locker room, one student organization office, two ticket offices, one ballroom, one multipurpose room, an outdoor patio, wireless access, an art gallery, six multicultural centers, one catering kitchen, and an underground service tunnel
Facilities renovated: Seven office spaces and a multicultural center

California State University–Northridge
Sol Center (renovation/addition)
Northridge, Calif.

In 1999, California State University–Northridge decided that it was time to consider upgrading its union facility. Since a budget was not provided to build a new facility, the university chose to renovate certain areas of the building and tear down others. After a two-phase renovation project, the Sol Center was completed.

According to Debra L. Hammond, executive director of Sol Center, the new building is completely handicap accessible, provides more space and resources for student organizations, and is eco-friendly.

"The design and construction processes were driven by students to support their expressed needs, as well as accessibility, sustainability, technology, energy efficiency, and responsible stewardship for the resources we are entrusted to use," Hammond said. "Not only is the resulting facility a tremendously useful student center, but also the intentional student involvement in the design and construction processes have supported the values of student engagement, development, and learning."

Submitted by: Debra L. Hammond, Executive Director
Full-time equivalent enrollment: 34,000
Four-year, public, urban
Opened: June 2006
Total gross area: 40,666 sq. ft.
Area renovated: 5,942 sq. ft.
Area added: 34,724 sq. ft.
Assignable area: 80%
Project cost: $15.2 million
Funding source: 100% student fees
Architect: Harley Ellis Devereaux – Los Angeles
Facilities added: Five medium meeting rooms, three small meeting rooms, one branded food concept, one quiet lounge, one television lounge, one information center, two computer labs, 28 office spaces, a coffee house, one student organization office, one student organization storage area, one ticket office, an outdoor patio, wireless access, student health resource room, and a bank
Facilities renovated: Pub, one office space, a ballroom, and one multipurpose room

Photos courtesy of Debra L. Hammond

85

Colorado State University
Lory Student Center Transit Center (renovation/addition)
Fort Collins, Colo.

In 2006, Colorado State University's Lory Student Center opened its Transit Center, an area built as a warm and safe place for students and community members to wait for buses.

"The Transit Center at Colorado State University is the front door of the campus. For many, this facility will be their first impression of the university," said Kris Folsom, marketing and public relations director. "It will serve as a transitional space between [Colorado State University] and Fort Collins and create a prominent connection with the community."

Throughout the construction process, the university worked closely with the architects, contractors, and construction management team to use as many green building practices as possible. This resulted in the university receiving a Silver Certification in Leadership in Energy and Environmental Design (LEED).

"Some of these initiatives included incorporating the use of natural light, using of nontoxic carpets and paints, conserving water use with low-flow fixtures, maximizing indoor air quality, and using native, low-water plant species in the landscaping," Folsom said. "Approximately 85 percent of construction waste was diverted from landfills and recycled for other uses."

Submitted by: Kris Folsom, Marketing and Public Relations Director
Full-time enrollment: 24,600
Four-year, public, urban
Reopened: August 2006
Area renovated: 8,821 sq. ft.
Area added: 13,179 sq. ft.
Assignable area: 66.3%
Project cost: $4.9 million
Funding source: 100% government
Architect: Coover-Clark Associates – Denver, Colo.
Facilities renovated: One large meeting room, a snack bar, bookstore, and eight office spaces
Facilities added: One large meeting room, two small meeting rooms, one information center, one computer lab, nine office spaces, one convenient store, one locker room, one student organization office, an outdoor patio, wireless access, and a general lounge

Photos courtesy of Clifford Scutella

Genesee Community College
Wolcott J. Humphrey III Student Union (new building)
Batavia, N.Y.

Previously, Genesee Community College did not have a union on campus. But after several student opinion surveys over the years mentioned the desire for such a facility, the college decided to build a union. "The student union was a needed space for our students to meet and socialize in," said Clifford Scutella, assistant dean for student life.

As the primary users of the facility, "Students had input in the entire process from development to the opening," said Scutella. "They had input in design and color as well as food and decorations. Their insight into how and why students will use the space has contributed significantly to the success of the current use of space."

And Scutella is pleased with the resulting Wolcott J. Humphrey III Student Union. "Our union sports a unique design of two squares off set with 20-foot open ceilings. The design is complemented only by the windows, skylights, and colors that present a bright open atmosphere," he said. "It presents what students can have, use, and respect at an affordable price. It's beautiful and functional and appreciated."

Submitted by: Clifford Scutella, Assistant Dean for Student Life
Full-time equivalent enrollment: 2,000
Two-year, public, rural
Opened: January 2006
Total gross area: 10,000 sq. ft.
Assignable area: 10%
Project cost: $1.8 million
Funding source: 75% government funding; 25% private funding
Architect: Joy, McCoola, Zilch, P.C. – Glen Falls, N.Y.
Facilities added: Six large meeting rooms, six medium meeting rooms, five snack bars, a television lounge, one computer lab, five offices, five student organization offices, 70 multipurpose rooms, one outdoor patio, and wireless access

Minnesota State University
Centennial Student Union (renovation)
Mankato, Minn.

When a maintenance study revealed some concerns in the games room area of Minnesota State University's Centennial Student Union, the decision was made to renovate the space.

"[Concerns included] water intrusion in the billiards area and the underground ventilation ducts, ADA accessibility of our bowling lanes, as well as the need to replace numerous interior finishes and reconstruct a television lounge that had been lost by a previous project," said Scott Hagebak, operations director.

Once the decision was made to do a renovation, the Union Board and Student Association coordinated and approved all plans, including meeting with the architects to agree upon a design.

"New Brunswick seating and enhanced cosmic bowling effects were added to the bowling lanes, the pool tables and all finishes were refurbished in the billiards area, and a new high definition double screen television lounge was installed," Hagebak said.

When the project was complete, the university was happy with the decision to take on the renovation and even more pleased with the success of the new games room.

"Ever since we first opened the doors to the games room almost 40 years ago, we have hosted academic classes in bowling and billiards which in turn have served as a feeder program for new users of the facility," Hagebak said. "This, combined with a marketing campaign aimed at student organizations and [Minnesota State] families has made our facility very successful and certainly helped justify the expenditure in this area."

Submitted by: Scott Hagebak, Operations Director
Full-time enrollment: 14,000
Four-year, public
Reopened: August 2006
Area renovated: 18,887 sq. ft.
Assignable area: 53%
Project cost: $1 million
Funding source: 100% student fees
Architect: Paulsen Architects – Mankato, Minn.
Facilities renovated: A games room, bowling lanes, outdoor equipment, and vending area
Facilities added: Television lounge

Photos courtesy of Scott Hagebak

Philadelphia University
Kanbar Campus Center (new building)
Philadelphia

Photos courtesy of Katie Tyler

Because the pre-existing college union was too small to accommodate a growing campus, leaving Philadelphia University students with no central socializing area, the university decided to construct a new building, the Kanbar Campus Center.

"The Kanbar Campus Center features an open design with walls of windows to capture the natural setting of Philadelphia University as well as make events visible from much of the main campus," said Katie Tyler, assistant director of student activities operations. "Dining options range from a café for snacks to facilities for formal parties. The second level has a coffee bar, billiards, flat screen television, comfortable lounge space, and convenience store for the university community. A performance center and display areas allow students to showcase their talents."

Students were very much involved in the planning process of the new union. From campus-wide committees to student-based discussions, every student on campus had a chance to give their opinion. And student leader approval was sought through the entire process.

The result is a facility that the whole university community can enjoy. "The Kanbar Campus Center is a new centerpiece for the Philadelphia University campus," Tyler said. "[It] is the anchor to the transforming main campus."

Submitted by: Katie Tyler, Assistant Director of Student Activities Operations
Full-time equivalent enrollment: 3,500
Four-year, private
Opened: September 2006
Total gross area: 75,235 sq. ft.
Assignable area: 60%
Project cost: $17 million
Funding source: 71% private funding; 29% government funding
Architect: Shelpley Bulfinch Richardson Abbott – Boston
Facilities added: Four medium meeting rooms, two small meeting rooms, one cafeteria, a bookstore, one quiet lounge, an information center, one computer lab, a games room, nine office spaces, one convenience store, a coffee house, one photo room, two student organization offices, one student organization storage area, one multipurpose room, two outdoor patios, wireless access, a copy center, mail services, three interview rooms, and a resource room

Photos by Jeff Goldberg, Esto Photographics

Phillips Exeter Academy
Phelps Academy Center (renovation)
Exeter, N.H.

Previous to 2006, Phillips Exeter Academy, a co-educational residential school for students in grades 9 through 12 and post-graduate levels, did not have a union or central building for meetings and socializing. But when the construction of a new science building left a vacated facility in the heart of campus, an opportunity arose.

"A planning committee of faculty, staff, and students was formed to decide the old building's fate," said Joanne Lembo, director of student activities. "The committee concluded that the old building should be the new Academy Center. The alumni affairs and development office raised $17 million in private donations, and an additional $10 million was raised for operational expenses."

Not only did the academy renovate the old building, but also the new union is LEED-registered (Leadership in Energy and Environmental Design), and a candidate for the LEED Silver designation, which designates standards for green or sustainable buildings. The Phelps Academy Center is the largest LEED building in New Hampshire [as of 2007].

Submitted by: Joanne G. Lembo, Director of Student Activities
Full-time equivalent enrollment: 1,062
Four-year, private, residential high school
Opened: April 2006
Total gross area: 49,236 sq. ft.
Assignable area: 85%
Project cost: $17 million
Funding source: 100% private funding
Architect: Centerbrook Architects and Planners – Centerbrook, N.H.
Facilities renovated: One multipurpose room, one large meeting room, two medium-sized meeting rooms, one small meeting room, one snack bar, a crafts shop, three music lounges, one auditorium, one reading lounge, one television lounge, three computer labs, a game room, eight office spaces, a convenient store, one locker room, ten student organization offices, one student organization storage area, wireless access, a radio station, a post office, and a kitchen

San Juan College
The Learning Commons (renovation)
Farmington, N.M.

With an ever-growing population, the existing union facility at San Juan College did not support students' needs. So, the university decided to build a new combined library and student activities area.

"The new library area provides an outstanding view of the surrounding mountains and beautiful southwest sunsets," said Rhonda Schaefer, public relations specialist. "Along with the state-of-the-art library, the student activities area is for student government, clubs, informal gatherings, quiet study rooms and meeting areas, computer workstations, as well as a student commons and game area."

Because the building is for the students, their opinions were taken into consideration every step of the way, resulting in The Learning Center, which provides an inviting environment for both the students and local community of San Juan College.

Submitted by: Rhonda Schaefer, Public Relations Specialist
Full-time enrollment: 4,500
Two-year, public
Reopened: April 2006
Total gross area: 38,000 sq. ft.
Assignable area: 84%
Project cost: $7.6 million
Funding source: 66% government; 34% institution
Architect: Dekker/Perich/Sabatini – Albuquerque, N.M.
Facilities added: Three multipurpose rooms, five medium-sized meeting rooms, one quiet lounge, four computer labs, a games room, ten office spaces, a coffee house, one student organization office, one student organization storage area, wireless access, an art gallery, and copy center

Photos courtesy of Rhonda Schaefer

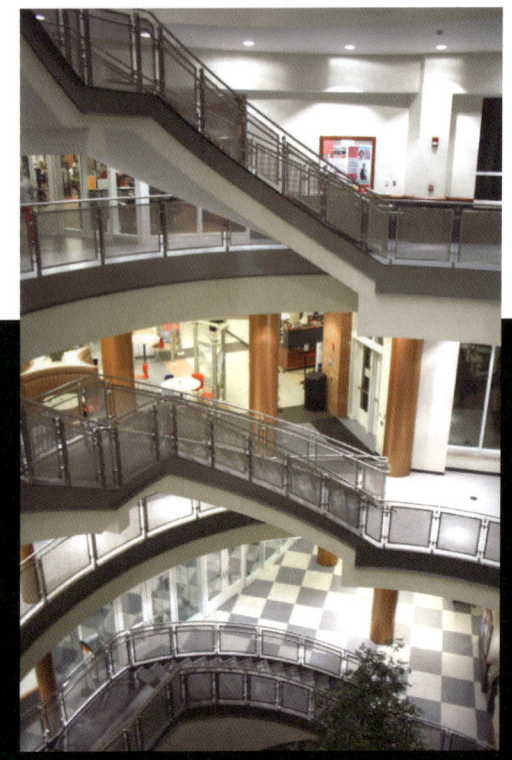

Photos courtesy of Brad Crerar

Southern Connecticut State University
Michael J. Adanti Student Center (new building)
New Haven, Conn.

In 1959, the Southern Connecticut State University constructed its first union as a residence hall and food service building. Over the years, students, staff, and faculty have tried to make the best of the space offered, but in 1996 the university knew that it was time for a change. After the decision was made to build a new union, the university turned to students, faculty, and staff to help make almost every decision.

"A very centralized location was picked as well as a majority of the amenities of the building," said Brad Crerar, director of the Adanti Student Center. "Students were continually assessed from 1996 through the opening of the building, January 2006, for important needs and changes to improve their campus life."

The university also turned to some other resources to assist the process. "The Adanti Student Center was built with a great deal of knowledge we received from various student centers and college unions," Crerar said. "We learned a great deal from educational tools such as 'From Blueprint to Reality,' as well as construction/building conferences, all sponsored by ACUI."

Now, Crear explains, that the year-old facility is able to accommodate the student population. "[There is] enough space for most of our clubs and organizations," he said. "Our meeting rooms on the top floor include catering set-up rooms that allow meetings to continue without interruption."

Crerar is proud to have the Adanti Student Center to offer to the students of the university. "We feel we have a state-of-the art building with a fine balance of tools and toys for our students to use. We have truly become the hearth and home of student life at Southern Connecticut State University," he said.

Submitted by: Brad Crerar, Director, Adanti Student Center
Full-time equivalent enrollment: 13,000
Four-year, public, urban
Opened: January 2006
Total gross area: 125,000 sq. ft.
Assignable area: 79%
Project cost: $28 million
Funding source: 100% student fees
Architect: Jeter Cook and Jepsen – Hartford, Conn.
Facilities added: Two multipurpose rooms, one large meeting room, 11 medium meeting rooms, seven small meeting rooms, two branded food venues, a bookstore, an auditorium with fixed seating, three reading lounges, one television lounge, one information center, two computer labs, a games room, 20 offices, two food service areas, a coffee house, a locker room, 13 student organization offices, two student organization storage areas, one ticket office, one ballroom, three fitness rooms, three outdoor patios, an art gallery, one multicultural center, a copy center, and wireless access

Texas Tech University
Student Union Building (renovation/addition)
Lubbock, Texas

After determining the union was outdated, students passed a referendum for a fee increase and Texas Tech University began plans to renovate its college union. Since their fees were funding the project, students were able to voice their opinions during planning and focus groups meetings, as well as be represented through the student government. And the university is quite pleased with the result.

"[Some of the unique features are] innovative use of limestone, views into and outside of building, artwork in building and landscaping, and artwork outside of the building," said Matthew Ducatt, managing director of student union and activities. "We believe we have a magnificent facility that offers students a wonderful environment in which to study, relax, eat, conduct meetings, and enjoy themselves while on the Texas Tech campus."

Submitted by: Matthew Ducatt, Managing Director, Student Union and Activities
Full-time equivalent enrollment: 27,996
Four-year, public
Opened: June 2006
Total gross area: 250,000 sq. ft.
Area renovated: 170,000 sq. ft.
Area added: 80,000 sq. ft.
Assignable area: 50%
Project cost: $45 million
Funding source: 100% student fees
Architect: Holzman Moss, Inc. – New York
Facilities added: Four medium meeting rooms, five small meeting rooms, three branded food concepts, one bookstore, a theater, one quiet lounge, two television lounges, four computer labs, nine office spaces, 64 cubicle offices for student organizations, a ticket office, an outdoor patio, wireless access, poster service, copy center, an ID office, a bank, and a cell phone center
Facilities renovated: Two large meeting rooms, five medium meeting rooms, seven small meeting rooms, a snack bar, a theater, faculty lounge, information center, a ballroom, an outdoor patio, and a post office

Photos by denmarsh photography

University of North Carolina–Wilmington
Fisher Student Center (new building)
Wilmington, N.C.

At the University of North Carolina–Wilmington, the college union could not meet the needs of the growing student body.

"The existing facilities provided many offices and service spaces, but had limited lounge and gathering spaces. Design of existing facilities did not facilitate the union distinguishing itself physically from other facilities," said Carolyn Farley, director of the Fisher Student Center. "The new building and anticipated renovations [to the old union] allow for more lounge space, a movie theater, and larger meeting spaces to accommodate our growing community."

Other features include student artwork displayed in meeting rooms and public areas throughout the building, as well as a memorial lounge created to commemorate the life of students who pass while attending the university.

The memorial lounge concept is one way that students participated in the planning of the new union. Through campus-wide surveys given from 1999–2001, students were able to voice opinions on the needs of the building. Also, the Union Advisory Board was involved in the picking of names for both meeting and lounge spaces and consulted in the review of interior finishes and furniture.

Farley and the university are proud of the new facility and want to share the school's experiences with others. "The architect and I have presented educational sessions on this project for many years in an effort to educate others on the process and challenges," she said.

Submitted by: Carolyn Farley, Director, Fisher Student Center
Full-time equivalent enrollment: 11,848
Four-year, public, urban
Opened: July 2006
Total gross area: 70,536 sq. ft.
Assignable area: 46%
Project cost: $31.8 million
Funding source: 82% student fees; 18% other
Architect: David Hatton of Burt Hill – Philadelphia
Facilities added: Two large meeting rooms, four medium meeting rooms, one small meeting room, one branded food cafeteria, one snack bar, a bookstore, a movie theater, one reading lounge, one information center, two computer labs, a game room, one office space, one locker room, three student organization offices, two student organization storage areas, one box office, two outdoor patios, wireless access, one alumni lounge, and a commuter student service area

Photos courtesy of Jodie Kern

Virginia Tech
Graduate Life Center (renovation)
Blacksburg, Va.

In the 1990s, Virginia Tech decided to invest more interest into graduate studies at the university by building the Graduate Life Center. After 10 years of planning, funds were finally allocated for the project, and the building designated for the renovation project was vacated.

"The renovation was done in two phases," said Jodie Kern, Graduate Life Center operations manager. "Two floors of the existing facility were renovated and currently house 36 graduate school offices, as well as conference and common areas. The interior aesthetics changed from a dark and gloomy setting to a bright and welcoming setting. The project was completed in three months, nearly impossible, but it happened. New carpeting, lighting, and wall coverings, not to mention technology, furniture, and offerings have assisted in making the [Graduate Life Center] the premier hub for graduate students."

The new Graduate Life Center was built with student and staff input, and the result is exactly what Virginia Tech wanted.

"This facility is the only facility in the nation to incorporate graduate social and meeting space with graduate school offices and graduate housing" Kern said. "Our motto is 'Building Graduate Community,' and we are well on our way."

Submitted by: Jodie Kern, Graduate Life Center Operations Manager
Full-time enrollment: 25,000
Four-year, public
Reopened: August 2006
Area renovated: 95,024 sq. ft.
Assignable area: 84%
Project cost: $4.7 million
Funding source: 40% student fees; 40% institution; 20% other
Architect: Robert (Bob) Boynton of Boynton, Rothschild, Rowland Architects — Richmond, Va.
Facilities renovated: One multipurpose room, 100 guest rooms, four medium meeting rooms, two small meeting rooms, an auditorium, one faculty lounge, one quiet lounge, one television lounge, one information center, one computer lab, 36 office spaces, a coffee house, one locker room, five student organization offices, one student organization storage area, wireless access, a copy center, a study room, and a career, health, and wellness room

Eastern Michigan University
EMU Student Center (new building)
Ypsilanti, Mich.

In 2001, Eastern Michigan University realized that the historic McKenny Union was too small to serve the campus community. During the following year, the decision was made to preserve and reassign the McKenny Union and construct a new college union that would accommodate the needs to the university. Since its opening, the EMU Student Center has lived up to expectations.

"EMU Student Center was a true undertaking of teamwork. Its success is specifically due to the students who dedicated themselves to the project through the years," said Carlos Costa, director. "With its high-performance building elements and design centered on the needs of the university community, this building will serve EMU and the surrounding community for years to come."

Submitted by: Carlos Costa, Director
Full-time enrollment: 16,393
Four-year, public, urban, commuter, residential
Opened: November 2006
Total area: 181,000 sq. ft.
Assignable space: 85%
Project cost: $40.4 million
Funding source: 83% student fees; 17% debt restructuring
Architect: Burt Hill Kosar Rittelmann – Philadelphia
Facilities added: Eight branded food concepts, an additional food area, three quiet lounges, television lounge, a patio, three multicultural centers, 6,960 sq. ft. suite to accommodate 40 student organizations, 105 sq. ft. student organization storage area, an information center, ticket office, three e-mail kiosks, one locker room, two art galleries, graphics services, bookstore, four retail stores, a games room, four small meeting rooms, nine medium meeting rooms, four large meeting rooms, one theater, two multi-purpose rooms, 19,965 sq. ft. of administrative office space with 11 offices, an admissions welcome center, one gender neutral/family bathroom, three kiva rooms, and wireless Internet access

Photos courtesy of Denmarsh Photoraphy

2008

American University

California State University–Dominguez Hills

Fort Hays State University

Florida International University

University of Iowa

University of Utah

Vanderbilt University

University of Vermont

Virginia Commonwealth University

University of Wisconsin–River Falls

renovation & construction SHOWCASE

Photo courtesy of Farrshid Assassi

California State University-Dominguez Hills | Loker Student Union | Carson, Calif.

Photos courtesy of Scott E. Jones

American University (renovation)
Mary Graydon Center
Washington, D.C.

SUBMITTED BY: Michael Elmore, Senior Director
FULL-TIME ENROLLMENT: 11,000
Four-year, private, urban, residential
REOPENED: August 2007
AREA RENOVATED: 22,900 sq. ft.
TOTAL AREA: 32,600 sq. ft.
ASSIGNABLE SPACE: 54%
PROJECT COST: $1.6 million
FUNDING SOURCE: 100% private donations
ARCHITECT: Kerns Group Architects – Arlington, Va.
FACILITIES RENOVATED: Quiet lounge, information center, multipurpose rooms, administrative office space, additional lounge, and installed wireless Internet access

American University renovated the first floor of the Mary Graydon Center in 2007. Improvements were to the aesthetics, including new furniture, flooring, lighting, and an emphasis on openness and flexibility.

"The renovation provided the opportunity to energize previously underutilized spaces such as the Tavern and the Corner Lounge," said Michael Elmore, senior director. "The open nature of the first floor and the flexibility of the furniture layout give students the freedom to use the spaces for casual lounging, group study, group meetings, and scheduled programming."

Sustainability also was a consideration during the renovation, as many of the finishes used were environmentally friendly.

California State University–Dominguez Hills (renovation/addition)
Loker Student Union
Carson, Calif.

SUBMITTED BY: Kim Clark, Executive Director
FULL-TIME ENROLLMENT: 8,764
Four-year, public, urban, commuter
RE-OPENED: January 2007
AREA ADDED: 53,302 sq. ft.
TOTAL AREA: 114,038 sq. ft.
ASSIGNABLE SPACE: 65%
PROJECT COST: $33.9 million
FUNDING SOURCE: 88% student fees; 12% private donations
ARCHITECT: Cannon Design – Los Angeles, Calif.
FACILITIES ADDED: Four branded food concepts, pub, three quiet lounges, four patios, multicultural center, accommodations for 28 student organizations, 100 sq. ft. student organization storage area, graphics services, copy center, two retail areas, three small meeting rooms, six medium meeting rooms, wireless Internet access
FACILITIES RENOVATED: Coffee shop, dining room, two food areas, quiet lounge, two patios, 3,000 sq. ft. student organization suite, information center, bookstore, games room, small meeting room, four medium meeting rooms, multipurpose area with three sections, 2,857 sq. ft. of administrative office space, and campus dining area

In 1999, the California State University–Dominguez Hills decided the existing union was too small to accommodate a growing campus population. So, a committee was established to start considering a renovation. Eight years later, the renovation and expansion project is complete.

"Because of the completeness of the renovation, the exterior of the old and the new are cohesive, as is the interior layout. New visitors to campus are not aware that the building includes a renovated area and an addition—they think of it as one space," said Kim Clark, executive director.

Clark also believes that the renovation project has brought new life to the union.

"This has been a true 'makeover' with significant impact on the way our students interact and relate. The existing building had become almost detrimental to student life in that it was too small to host anything significant. The renovation and expansion has provided a much needed focal point for students and created a new sense of community," she said.

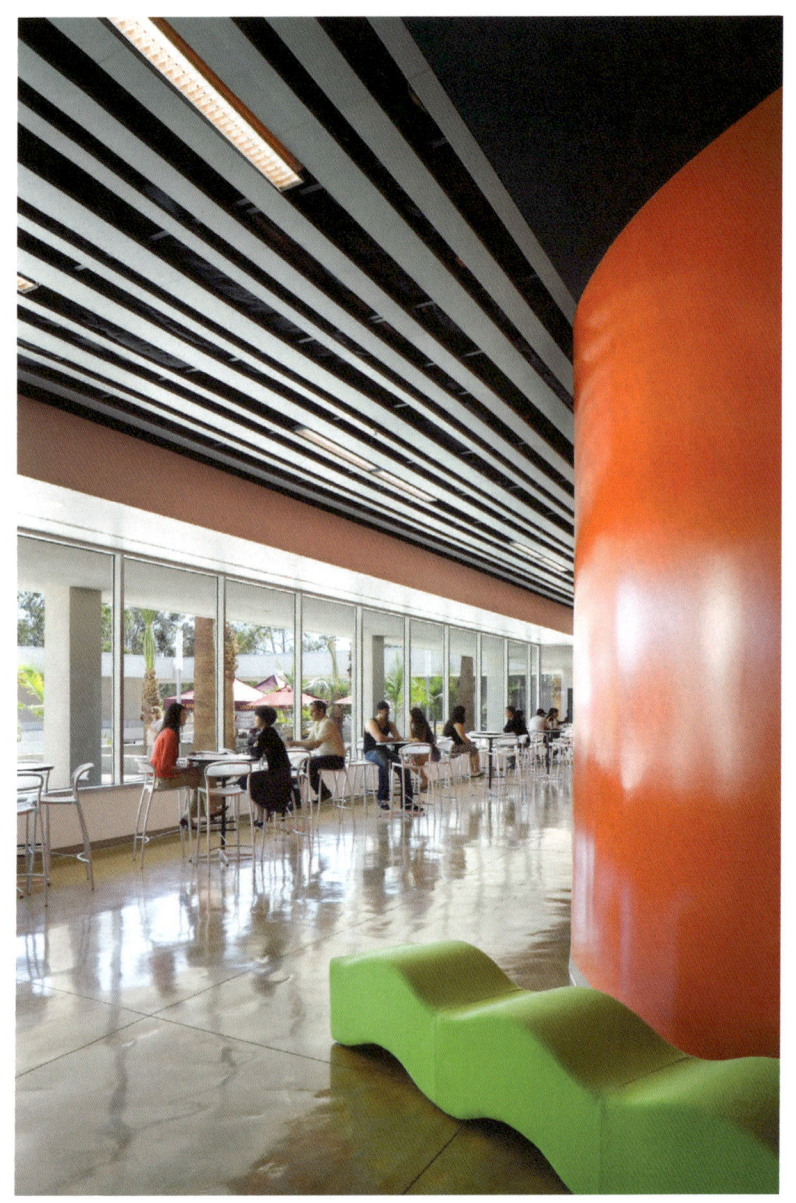

Fort Hays State University (renovation/addition)
Memorial Union
Hays, Kan.

SUBMITTED BY: Bill Smriga, Director
FULL-TIME ENROLLMENT: 6,031
Four-year, public, rural
RE-OPENED: August 2007
AREA ADDED: 4,739 sq. ft.
TOTAL AREA: 101,495 sq. ft.
ASSIGNABLE SPACE: 60%
PROJECT COST: $8.5 million
FUNDING SOURCE: 75% student fees; 15% institution funding; 5% contributions from Chartwells and Barnes & Noble
ARCHITECT: Howard & Helmer – Wichita, Kan.
FACILITIES ADDED: Quiet lounge, two small meeting rooms, one medium meeting room, one large meeting room, and installed wireless Internet access
FACILITIES RENOVATED: Branded food concept, dining room, quiet lounge, television lounge, nightclub, patio, multicultural center, 4,132 sq. ft. student organization suite, 136 sq. ft. student organization storage area, graphics services, copy center, bookstore, information center, games room, retail area, four small meeting rooms, two medium meeting rooms, one large meeting room, two multipurpose rooms, and 904 sq. ft. of administrative office space

The Memorial Union at Fort Hays State University had not been renovated since 1968.

"The principal desired outcome of the project was to once again transform the Memorial Union into a destination point for students," said Bill Smriga, director.

Smriga said the renovation was a success, especially with the addition of state-of-the-art technology.

"The before and after pictures of the union are dramatic. The renovation features the best ideas of about 10 different union buildings visited during the planning process," Smriga said.

Florida International University (addition)
Biscayne Bay Campus Fitness Center
North Miami, Fla.

SUBMITTED BY: Christina Fisher, Coordinator
FULL-TIME ENROLLMENT: 38,000
Four-year, public
RE-OPENED: October 2007
TOTAL AREA: 144,500 sq. ft.
ASSIGNABLE SPACE: 7%
PROJECT COST: $3.5 million
FUNDING SOURCE: 15% institution funding; 85% capital improvement trust fund
ARCHITECT: Hanbury Evans Wright Vlattas – Tampa, Fla.
FACILITIES ADDED: Food area, patio, student organization storage area, fitness center, locker room, and an administrative office

The students of Florida International University requested an improvement to the fitness center. "The previous work-out room was a 300-square-foot facility located on the third floor of the Wolfe University Center," said Christina Fisher, coordinator. While the location was "efficient," according to Fisher, many of the auxiliary needs, such as water fountains, restrooms, and administrative space were scattered.

The new Biscayne Bay Campus Fitness Center takes care of all of these problems. "Our new fitness center now houses a cardio village, women's and men's locker room, free weight area, an aerobics room with a dance floor and stretching bar, storage, a copy center, conference room, and all of the Biscayne Bay Campus Recreation Administration," Fisher said.

The university now has an accessible, central location for its campus community fitness center.

Photos courtesy of Christina Fisher

University of Iowa (renovation/addition)
Iowa Memorial Union
Iowa City, Iowa

SUBMITTED BY: Nancy Abram, Marketing and Design Manager
FULL-TIME ENROLLMENT: 30,402
Four-year, public, rural, residential
REOPENED: January 2007
AREA ADDED: 13,000 sq. ft.
TOTAL AREA: 325,000 sq. ft.
ASSIGNABLE SPACE: 70%
PROJECT COST: $9.9 million
FUNDING SOURCE: 100% student fees
ARCHITECT: Burt Hill Kosar Rittelmann – Philadelphia; OPN – Cedar Rapids, Iowa
FACILITIES RENOVATED: Branded food concept, quiet lounge, television lounge, patio, student organization suite, student organization storage area, information center, ticket office, art gallery, copy center, bookstore, theater, multipurpose room, and installed wireless Internet access

This renovation was the fifth completed on the Iowa Memorial Union since it was built in 1925.

"The goals of the project were to improve wayfinding in the building, increase student lounge and gathering space, improve the office space for student organizations, enhance the relationship of the building with the Iowa Rives, and take care of some deferred maintenance in certain areas," said Nancy Abram, marketing and design manager.

A noteworthy feature born out of the renovation was the expansion of the River Patio to include a River Terrace and Riverfront stage for student and public gatherings.

University of Utah (renovation)
A. Ray Olpin University Union
Salt Lake City, Utah

Photos by Branden Dalley

SUBMITTED BY: Branden Dalley, Associate Director
FULL-TIME ENROLLMENT: 28,000
Four-year, public, commuter
RE-OPENED: September 2007
AREA RENOVATED: 1,650 sq. ft.
ASSIGNABLE SPACE: 100%
PROJECT COST: $100,000
FUNDING SOURCE: 100% institution
ARCHITECT: Charles Gaddis – Salt Lake City
FACILITIES RENOVATED: Student lounge

The new Crimson Lounge at the University of Utah offers something for everyone, according to Branden Dalley, associate director. Features of the lounge include a student-run art gallery that displays work of local artists and a plasma screen television with more than 120 international channels in their respective languages. "The international component to the lounge fits in perfectly with our current mission of the university: to reach out to our international population," Dalley said.

The lounge is split into two areas, one for studying and one for socializing. "Our lounge is a perfect example of offering to our students what they want. The lounge is a big hit," Dalley said.

Vanderbilt University
Commons Center (new building)
Nashville, Tenn.

SUBMITTED BY: Jack Davis, Director of Student Centers
Full-time enrollment: 6,200
Four-year, private, urban, residential
OPENED: August 2007
TOTAL AREA: 114,088 sq. ft.
ASSIGNABLE SPACE: 68%
PROJECT COST: $25 million
FUNDING SOURCE: 100% institution
ARCHITECT: Bruner/Cott & Associates – Cambridge, Mass.
FACILITIES ADDED: Snack bar, cafeteria, coffee shop, two quiet lounges, a television lounge, three patios, an information center, four e-mail kiosk stations, a fitness center, graphic services, copy center, games room, two small meeting rooms, one medium meeting room, one large meeting room, one multipurpose room with two sections, 2,000 sq. ft. of administrative office space, seven administrative offices, dining hall, post office, writing studio, and wireless Internet connectivity

In 2008, first-year students had the opportunity to be a part of a new concept at Vanderbilt University, with the Commons Center as the "center piece," according to Jack Davis, director of student centers. The Commons Center is a place "where faculty, students, and educational professionals interact as a community," he said.

The Commons consists of 10 new or renovated residence halls, a dean's residence, and the Commons Center. According to Davis, the Commons Center is a state-of-the-art building and received a LEED Silver rating.

"Many aspects of the project were based on sustainable design and were closely monitored during the construction process," he said. "The center focuses on recycling, including no 'to go' containers from the dining hall."

The Commons Center was one of Tenneessee's first LEED-certified buildings.

Photos by Richard Mandelkorn

University of Vermont (new building)
Dudley H. Davis Center
Burlington, Vt.

SUBMITTED BY: Kate Strotmeyer, Marketing Coordinator
FULL-TIME ENROLLMENT: 9,040
Four-year, public
OPENED: October 2007
TOTAL AREA: 186,000 sq. ft.
ASSIGNABLE SPACE: 70%
PROJECT COST: $61 million
FUNDING SOURCE: 80% student fees; 2% institution funding; 4% private donations; 14% income activities (retail and conference rentals)
ARCHITECT: WTW Architects – Pittsburgh; Truex Collins & Partners Architects – Burlington, Vt.
FACILITIES ADDED: Three branded food concepts, cafeteria, pub, coffee shop, five quiet lounges, nightclub, patio, multicultural center, 3,200 sq. ft. student organization suite, 1,660 sq. ft. student organization storage area, two information centers, 15 e-mail kiosks, art gallery, graphics services, copy center, bookstore, six retail areas, games room, four small meeting rooms, three medium meeting rooms, two multipurpose rooms, 3,800 sq. ft. of administrative office space, and wireless Internet access

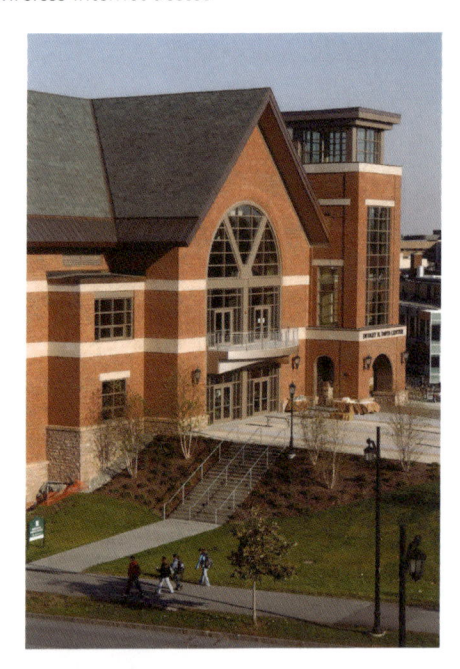

Prior to the opening of the Dudley H. Davis Center, the University of Vermont lacked a true college union. Rather, the university had converted an old library into a union; but, according to Kate Strotmeyer, marketing coordinator, this building's atmosphere was not ideal. So, the decision was made to construct a new building.

"The Davis Center is unusual in the amount of local Vermont products that were used to construct the building, from its Vermont slate roof to its Vermont brick exterior. The building also used a significant amount of material that was recycled from the structures that were deconstructed to make way for it," Strotmeyer said.

Also, due to its energy-efficient design, the Davis Center is LEED certified.

Photos courtesy of Bob Handelman, Jeffrey Wakefield

Photos courtesy of Timothy Reed

Virginia Commonwealth University (renovation)
Hunton Student Center
Richmond, Va.

SUBMITTED BY: Timothy Reed, Director
FULL-TIME ENROLLMENT: 31,000
Four-year, public, urban
REOPENED: January 2007
TOTAL AREA: 24,891 sq. ft.
ASSIGNABLE SPACE: 47%
PROJECT COST: $5.5 million
FUNDING SOURCE: 95% student fees; 5% alumni association
ARCHITECT: Einhorn, Yaffee, Prescott Architecture and Engineering – Washington, D.C.
FACILITIES ADDED: Branded food concept, four student organization suites, information center, e-mail kiosk station, games room, eight small meeting rooms, one administrative office, building manager office, University Student Commons and Activities operations office, Learning Center office, and wireless Internet access
FACILITIES RENOVATED: Quiet lounge area and television lounge

According to Timothy Reed, director, the renovation of Hunton Student Center was unique.

"Hunton Student Center is a one-of-a-kind project where a historic structure was totally renovated to recreate a specialized campus center," he said. "The project preserved the integrity of a feature of Richmond history [and] became a modern centerpiece for student life at Virginia Commonwealth University."

The renovation maintained some of the original church building design including "nested" pews in the balcony, while still allowing some modern changes, such as replacing mechanical systems to improve efficiency.

Photos courtesy of Cara Rubis

University of Wisconsin–River Falls (new building)
University Center
River Falls, Wis.

SUBMITTED BY: Cara Rubis, Associate Director
FULL-TIME ENROLLMENT: 6,450
Four-year, public
OPENED: January 2007
TOTAL AREA: 142,660 sq. ft.
ASSIGNABLE SPACE: 48%
PROJECT COST: $34 million
FUNDING SOURCE: 97% student fees; 1% state government; 2% institution funding
ARCHITECT: Workshop Architects, Inc. – Milwaukee, Wis.; Moody Nolan – Columbus, Ohio
FACILITIES ADDED: Cafeteria, coffee shop, four other food areas, two quiet lounges, television lounge, nightclub, two patios, accommodations for 165 student organizations, two information centers, 35 e-mail kiosks, locker room, art gallery, graphics services, two copy centers, bookstore, two retail areas, three game rooms, outdoor equipment area, guest room, four small meeting rooms, five medium meeting rooms, two large meeting rooms, theater, two multipurpose rooms with three sections, 11,670 sq. ft. administrative office space, and wireless Internet connectivity

Originally, the University of Wisconsin–River Falls did not intend to build a new college union; rather, the institution planned to add onto the Hagestad Student Center to accommodate a growing student population. However, plans soon changed.

"The old student center lacked space for student programming, and it no longer met the needs of the students," said Cara Rubis, associate director. "After taking into consideration the long-term goals of the university—sustainability, diversity, community involvement, student services, and a recruitment tool—the only option that met these needs was to build a new University Center."

Driven by student recommendation, many features of the new University Center are green, such as water-efficient landscaping and sustainable cleaning systems. The building also received a LEED Silver rating.

2009

Creighton University

Mississippi State University

University of Wisconsin–Parkside

Weber State University

Indiana University-Purdue University–Indianapolis

University of Texas–San Antonio

University of the Pacific

Edinboro University of Pennsylvania

Kalamazoo College

University of Wisconsin–Stevens Point

Northern Kentucky University

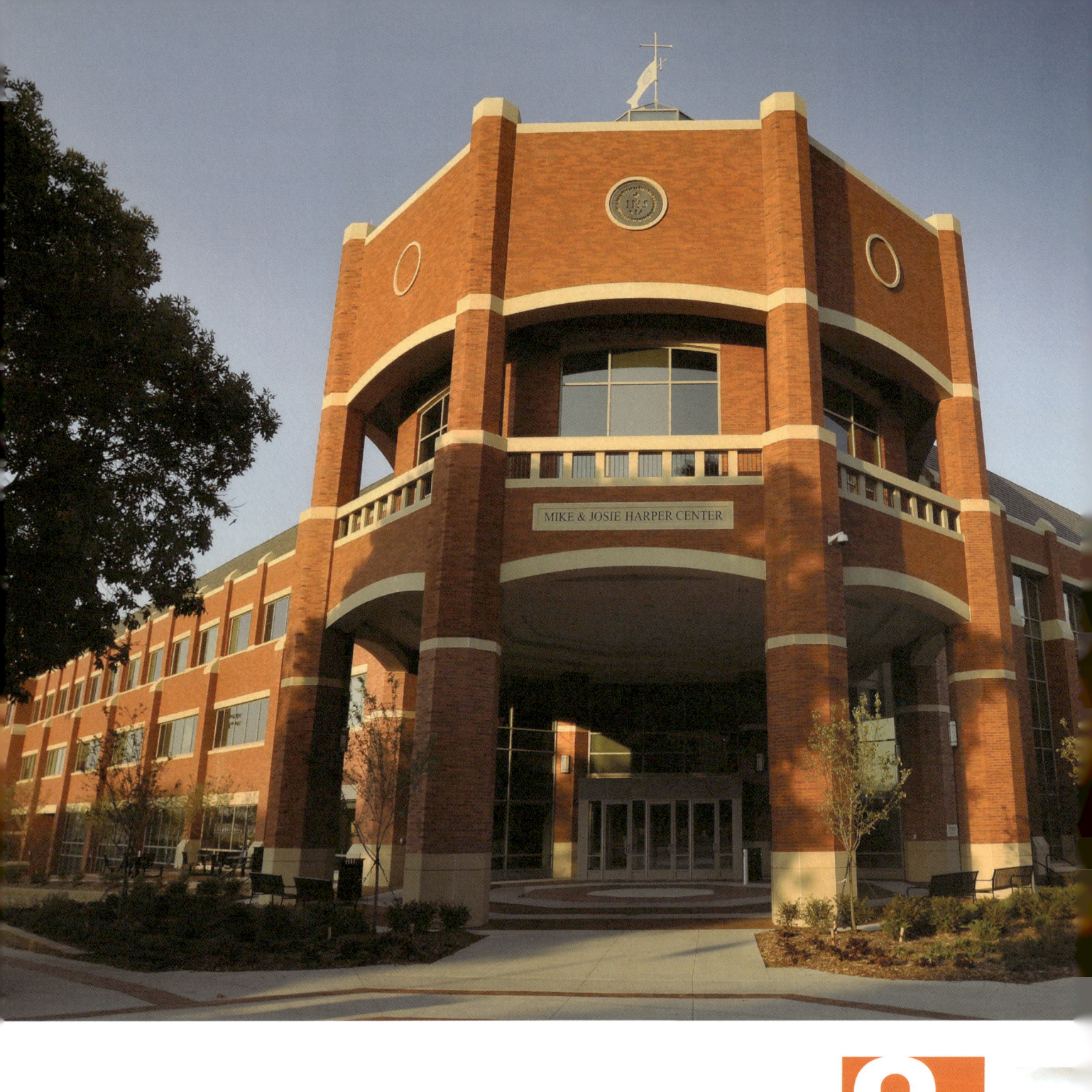

RENOVATION & CONSTRUCTION SHOWCASE

Creighton University (new building)
Harper Center for Student Life and Learning
Omaha, Neb.

SUBMITTED BY: Rowland W. Hughes, Director
Four-year, private, religious-affiliated
FULL-TIME ENROLLMENT: 6,576
OPENED: August 2008
TOTAL AREA: 245,658 sq. ft.
FLOORS: 4
ASSIGNABLE SPACE: 58%
PROJECT COST: $54.5 million
FUNDING SOURCE: 100% private donations
ARCHITECT: Opus Architects & Engineers – Minnetonka, Minn.
FACILITIES ADDED: Pub, dining room, three other food areas, three quiet lounges, three patios, multicultural center, information center, fitness center, locker room, bookstore, retail area, six small meeting rooms, four medium meeting rooms, two large meeting rooms, theater, four multipurpose rooms, 16 administrative offices, and wireless Internet access

The Mike and Josie Harper Center for Student Life and Learning serves as a landmark for Creighton University.

"The Harper Center is the nucleus of Creighton's dynamic eastward expansion and campus transformation uniting academic and student life services under one roof," said Rowland Hughes, director.

Bringing synergy to campus, the Harper Center now houses 16 university offices previously scattered, is a one-stop shop for prospective students, and combines social life with retail, life wellness, and educational opportunities.

"The facility links all components of the Creighton family together plus reinforces the university's vital standing within the Omaha, state, and national focus," Hughes said.

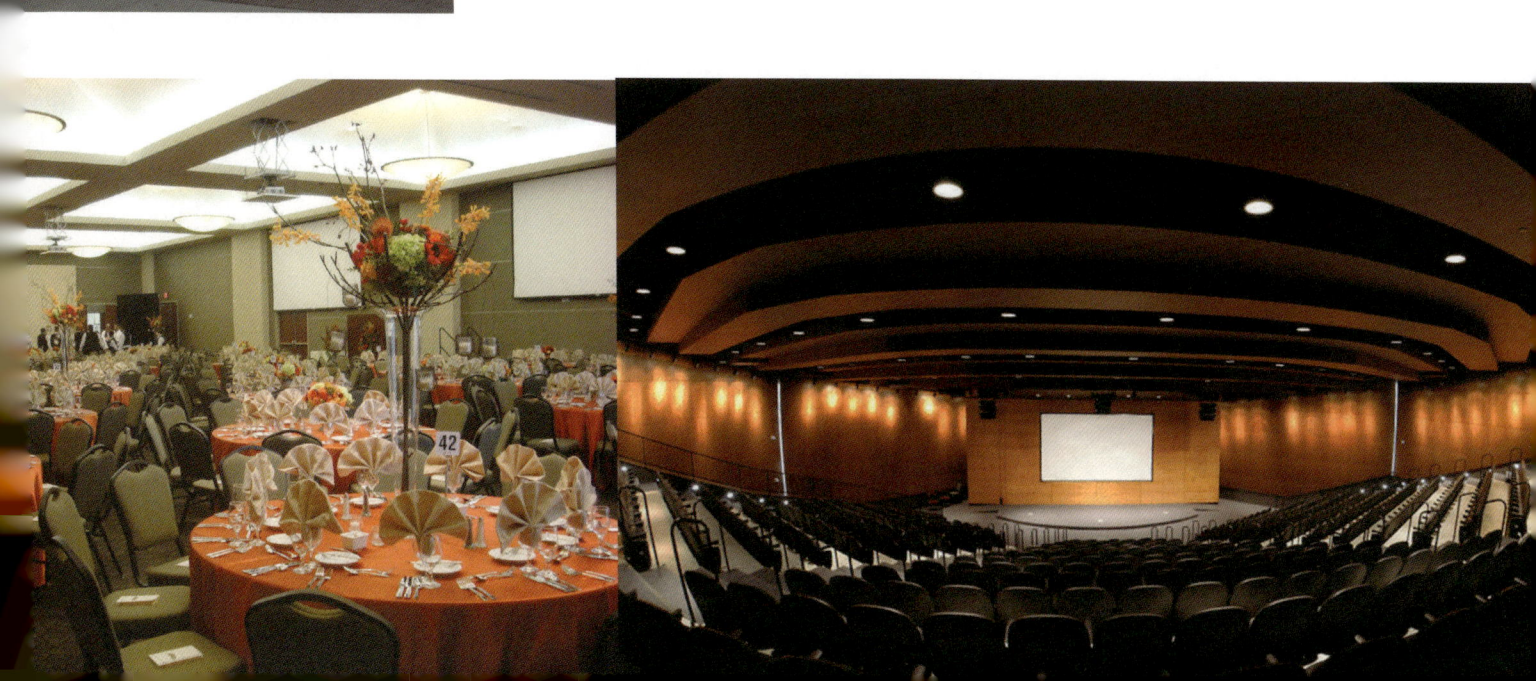

Mississippi State University (renovation/addition)
Colvard Student Union
Mississippi State, Miss.

Mississippi State University's Colvard Student Union needed a renovation and addition. It was not meeting ADA and fire safety codes, it was not large enough for the increased student body, and it was not meeting the needs of the student body. So, a consultant was hired, students and staff started touring recently renovated unions, and the renovation began.

"The old building was totally renovated and a 17,000-sq.-ft. addition was attached," said Edwin M. Keith Jr., director. "Codes were met, and the number, variety, and size of meeting rooms were expanded."

The new union is more student-friendly and serves the entire campus.

"The Colvard Student Union is a modern facility the embraces and blends well with the history and traditions of the state's land grant campus," Keith said.

SUBMITTED BY: Edwin M. Keith Jr., Director
Four-year, public, rural, residential
FULL-TIME ENROLLMENT: 14,469
ORIGINALLY OPENED: September 1964
REOPENED: January 2008
AREA ADDED: 17,000 sq. ft.
TOTAL AREA: 114,000 sq. ft.
FLOORS: 3
ASSIGNABLE SPACE: 60%
PROJECT COST: $23.5 million
FUNDING SOURCE: 64% government funding; 27% student fees; 9% institution funding
ARCHITECT: JH&H Architects – Jackson, Miss.
FACILITIES RENOVATED: Branded food concept, coffee shop, quiet lounge, patio, five student organization offices, information center, e-mail kiosk, theater, multipurpose room, three administrative offices, board room, and broadened wireless Internet access
FACILITIES ADDED: Four branded food concepts, other food area, quiet lounge, television lounge, patio, multicultural center, 15 student organization offices, three student organization storage areas, information center, gallery, copy center, retail area, small meeting room, two administrative offices, board room, two conference rooms, and main lounge

Photos courtesy of JH&H Architects Planners Interiors, P.A.

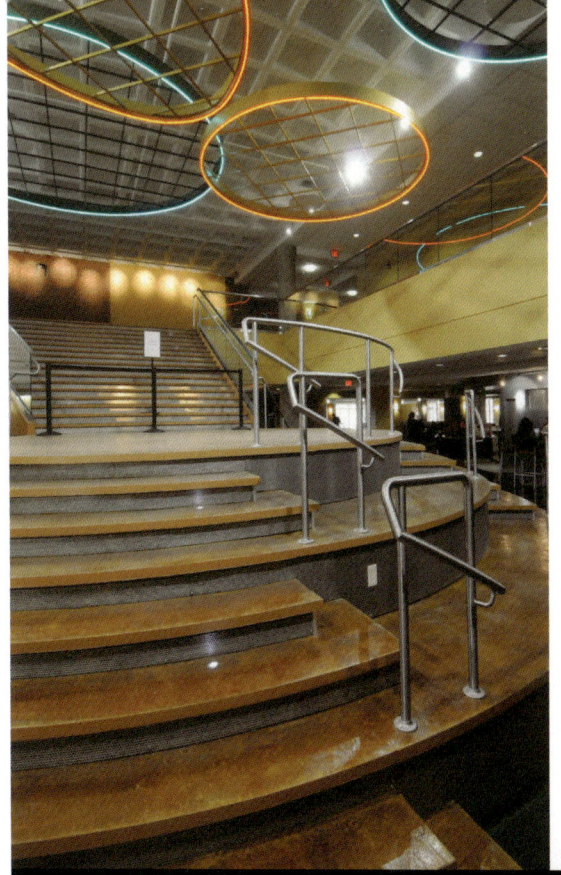

University of Wisconsin–Parkside (renovation/addition)
Student Center
Kenosha, Wis.

SUBMITTED BY: DeAnn Possehl, Director of Student Life
Four-year, public, urban, commuter
FULL-TIME ENROLLMENT: 3,600
ORIGINALLY OPENED: September 1976
REOPENED: December 2008
AREA RENOVATED: 68,942 sq. ft.
AREA ADDED: 53,075 sq. ft.
TOTAL AREA: 124,675 sq. ft.
FLOORS: 4
ASSIGNABLE SPACE: 62%
PROJECT COST: $24 million
FUNDING SOURCE: 94% student fees; 6% government funding
ARCHITECTS: WTW Architects – Pittsburgh, Penn.; KahlerSlater – Milwaukee, Wis.
FACILITIES RENOVATED: Cafeteria, other food area, television lounge, nightclub, 20 student organization offices, information center, ticket office, e-mail kiosk, games room, theater, and two administrative offices
FACILITIES ADDED: Coffee house, quiet lounge, two patios, student organization suite, student organization storage area, bookstore, three small meeting rooms, three medium meeting rooms, one large meeting room, multipurpose room, admissions center, and wireless Internet access

The Student Center at the University of Wisconsin–Parkside was not meeting all of the campus's needs.

"It was grossly undersized for the size of the campus and the growing residence hall population [and] had outdated dining facilities and aging infrastructure," said DeAnn Possehl, director of student life.

The university completed a facility audit and identified campus-wide needs to begin the planning process for the building's renovation. One need discovered was a gateway for the campus.

"The Student Center, along with the pedestrian mall that was created as part of the project, has created a front door for our campus," Possehl said. "The inclusion of a grand staircase has added a unique way-finding element to the facility that also serves as an entertainment platform and lounge. All of the areas of the Student Center flow in a very synergetic way."

And while the project combined a new structure and old, Possehl believes the difference cannot be seen.

"In our case, the architects did a wonderful job of 'fusing' these two elements into a cohesive building," she said.

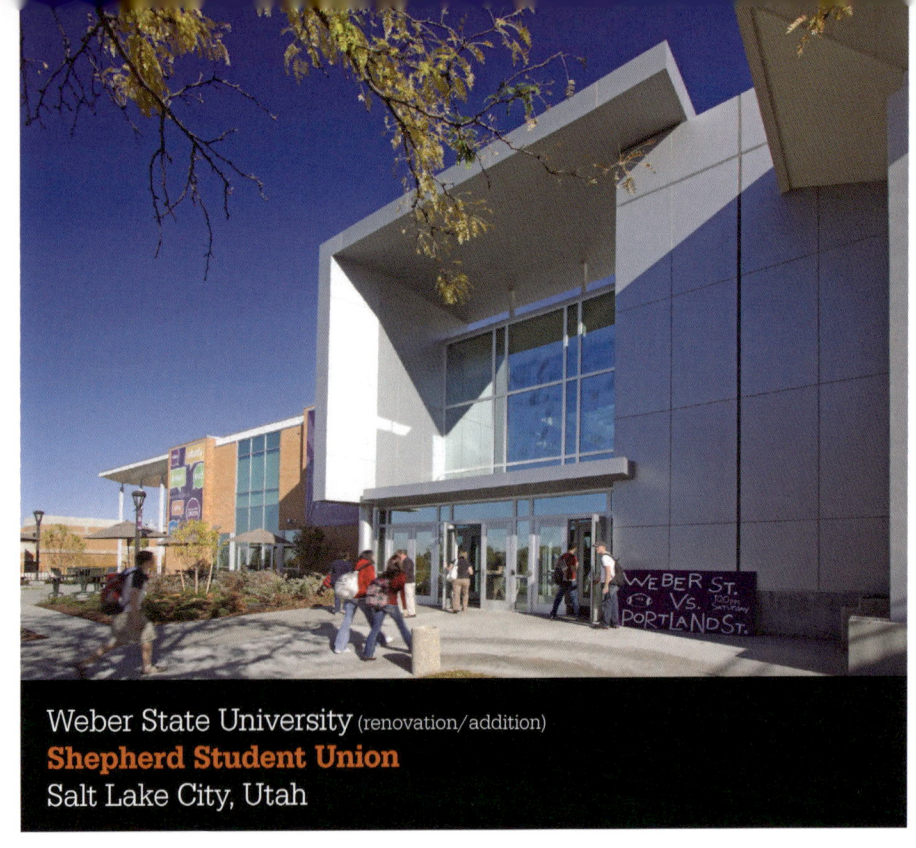

Weber State University (renovation/addition)
Shepherd Student Union
Salt Lake City, Utah

Weber State University's Shepherd Student Union had been pieced together over many years and was not a connected, easy-to-navigate place. The major goal of this renovation and addition was to unify and revitalize the building.

"The facility has come full circle from a disconnected and closed environment to a vibrant light-filled crossroads of campus life, where transparency and flexibility have been employed as tools to foster increased activity and inspire cross-program collaboration," said Liz Pulu, marketing coordinator.

During the renovation, however, the building's exterior was kept to "honor the building's original modern era design," Pulu said. "And because the campus sits on the foothills of the Wasatch Range, the design maximizes the building's connections with its beautiful mountainside setting."

SUBMITTED BY: Liz Pulu, Marketing Coordinator
Private, commuter
FULL-TIME ENROLLMENT: 21,000
ORIGINALLY OPENED: February 1960
REOPENED: August 2008
AREA ADDED: 21,026 sq. ft.
TOTAL AREA: 188,952 sq. ft.
FLOORS: 4
ASSIGNABLE SPACE: 58%
PROJECT COST: $23.6 million
FUNDING SOURCE: 100% student fees
ARCHITECTS: MHTN Architects, Inc. – Salt Lake City
FACILITIES RENOVATED: Branded food concept area, snack bar, cafeteria, dining room, quiet lounge, patio, student organization suite, multicultural center, information center, e-mail kiosk, gallery, child care center, graphics shop, copy center, bookstore, retail area, bowling lanes, games room, outdoor equipment area, large meeting room, theater, multipurpose room, administrative offices, and wireless Internet access

Photos courtesy of Zone VII Photography, Preston Norris

Indiana University-Purdue University–Indianapolis (new building)
Campus Center
Indianapolis, Ind.

SUBMITTED BY: Dan Maxwell, Director
Four-year, public, urban, commuter
FULL-TIME ENROLLMENT: 30,000
OPENED: January 2008
TOTAL AREA: 260,000 sq. ft.
FLOORS: 5
ASSIGNABLE SPACE: 59%
PROJECT COST: $56 million
FUNDING SOURCE: 18% government funding; 11% student fees; 71% institution funding
ARCHITECTS: SmithGroup – Washington, D.C.; Ratio Architects – Indianapolis, Ind.
FACILITIES ADDED: Branded food concepts, two cafeterias, two coffee shops, quiet lounge, television lounge, two patios, student organization suite, information center, ticket office, five e-mail kiosks, lockers, gallery, graphics shop, bookstore, retail space, games room, four small meeting rooms, three medium meeting rooms, five large meeting rooms, theater, multipurpose room with three sections, eight administrative offices, post office, ID card operations, credit union, and wireless Internet access

When Indiana University-Purdue University–Indianapolis was founded 20 years ago, constructing a union was in the plans. Finally, in 2002, the construction of the Campus Center was approved, and construction began in 2005.

"The Campus Center is in the heart of campus and has, in a very short time, begun to tweak the culture of the campus, the experience our students have, and [it's] making an impact on attracting new students to the campus," said Dan Maxwell, director.

As a new campus feature, the union is able to offer a central location for the university's primarily commuter students.

"Prior to the Campus Center, it was not uncommon for folks to eat their lunch in their cars, drive on and off campus multiple times in one day, and not have a real connection to the campus," Maxwell said. "We now find students, faculty, and staff here seven days a week, whether to meet up, grab something to eat, attend a meeting or an activity, relax, catch a nap, or engage in the true essence of IUPUI."

Photos courtesy of University of Texas–San Antonio

The University of Texas–San Antonio (new building)
University Center
San Antonio, Texas

SUBMITTED BY: John Kaulfus, Associate Dean of Students
Four-year, public, urban, residential
FULL-TIME ENROLLMENT: 28,500
OPENED: August 2008
TOTAL AREA: 65,000 sq. ft.
ASSIGNABLE SPACE: 60%
PROJECT COST: $25 million
FUNDING SOURCE: 100% student fees
ARCHITECT: Perkins+Will – Atlanta
FACILITIES ADDED: Cafeteria, coffee shop, Subway, quiet lounge, television lounge, patio, 14,000-sq.-ft. student organization suite, student organization storage area, information center, graphics shop, games room, two small meeting rooms, two medium meeting rooms, three large meeting rooms, multipurpose room with two sections, administrative office space, and wireless Internet access

Despite a small construction budget, the new University Center at the University of Texas–San Antonio was still able to meet all the campus needs.

"The needs of the facility were: expanded meeting space, conference space, student organizations space, food service space, and commuter lounge space. The facility design increased meeting space, conference space, student organization space, and lounge space, and provided more food venues," said John Kaulfus, associate dean of students.

And as the funding for the project came entirely from student fees, students had a say when it came to the building.

"Students were involved in every phase of this project from the selection of the architects to choosing the furniture through numerous town hall meetings and focus groups," Kaulfus said.

Overall, Kaulfus said, the University Center design is "one of a kind and offered custom solutions for the students of the campus."

University of the Pacific (new building)
Don and Karen DeRosa University Center
Stockton, Calif.

SUBMITTED BY: Jamie L. O'Regan, Assistant Director for Operations
Four-year, private, urban, commuter
FULL-TIME ENROLLMENT: 4,246
OPENED: August 2008
TOTAL AREA: 60,000 sq. ft.
FLOORS: 2
ASSIGNABLE SPACE: 75%
PROJECT COST: $40 million
FUNDING SOURCE: 50% private donations; 50% borrowed
ARCHITECT: Gensler – San Francisco, Calif.
FACILITIES ADDED: Snack bar, cafeteria, pub, coffee shop, dining room, faculty club, two patios, information center, four e-mail kiosks, bookstore, games room, two small meeting rooms, four medium meeting rooms, large meeting room, multipurpose room with two sections, 3,200-sq.-ft. administrative office space, and wireless Internet access

University of the Pacific did not have a true union, and it was in need.

"The construction of this facility has completely changed the campus dynamic in a positive light," said Jamie O'Regan, assistant director for operations.

A LEED Silver-certified building, the DeRosa University Center is green from top to bottom, including the shirts that staff wear, which are made from bamboo and charcoal technology.

As a symbol of innovation, the building features a retractable roof in both the common eating area and pub. O'Regan said students "wanted the building to feel connected to the outside," so, in addition to the roof, lots of windows also were included to infuse natural light.

"We want other campuses to understand that even after a facility is built, it is a living entity of the campus, and we need to continue to educate on responsibility in food, alcohol, and living," O'Regan said.

Photos by Mike Petrillo

SUBMITTED BY: Kari Althof, Assistant Director
Four-year, public
FULL-TIME ENROLLMENT: 7,700
ORIGINALLY OPENED: September 1971
REOPENED: January 2008
AREA RENOVATED: 41,084 sq. ft.
AREA ADDED: 47,199 sq. ft.
TOTAL AREA: 124,533 sq. ft.
FLOORS: 3
ASSIGNABLE SPACE: 95%
PROJECT COST: $21.2 million
FUNDING SOURCE: 100% student fees
ARCHITECT: WTW Architects – Pittsburgh, Penn.
FACILITIES RENOVATED: Cafeteria, two television lounges, multicultural center, student organization suite, information center, e-mail kiosk, two locker rooms, retail space, outdoor equipment area, one small meeting room, three medium meeting rooms, two large meeting rooms, administrative office space, and a gymnasium
FACILITIES ADDED: Coffee venue, two quiet lounges, two television lounges, patio, fitness center, games room, theater, multipurpose room, gymnasium, two aerobics studios, and wireless Internet access

Edinboro University of Pennsylvania (renovation/addition)
Frank G. Pogue Student Center
Edinboro, Penn.

Originally built in 1971, Edinboro University of Pennsylvania's Student Center completed an addition in 1994; however, according to Assistant Director Kari Althof, the building was in need of a facelift and another expansion.

"Students desired a coffee shop, theater, more recreation facilities, and updated restrooms," she said. "In addition, they wanted a building that was relaxing and in which they could feel at home."

Since the students had an invested interest in the building, their input was sought throughout the process.

"Students were involved in the project process from beginning to end," Althof said. "Keeping the students involved in the entire process was very much a priority for the university."

The end result was a building of which the whole campus could be proud.

"This was one of the most exciting projects that has been completed at Edinboro, especially because it was so student-focused," Althof said. "Our building can finally be used to its fullest potential and is continuing to grow and develop into a place where students and guests can feel at home."

Photos courtesy of Keith Mumma Photography

Kalamazoo College (renovation/addition)
Weimer K. Hicks Student Center
Kalamazoo, Mich.

SUBMITTED BY: Kate Leishman, Assistant Director of Student Activities
Four-year, private, residential
FULL-TIME ENROLLMENT: 1,300
REOPENED: September 2008
AREA RENOVATED: 72,000 sq. ft.
AREA ADDED: 6,000 sq. ft.
FLOORS: 3
ASSIGNABLE SPACE: 15%
PROJECT COST: $14.6 million
FUNDING SOURCE: 100% private donations
ARCHITECTS: Tower Pinkster – Kalamazoo, Mich.
FACILITIES RENOVATED: Cafeteria, dining room, other food area, patio, student organization suite, information center, e-mail kiosk, bookstore, games room, multipurpose room, 15 administrative offices, and mail center
FACILITIES ADDED: Coffee shop, television lounge, student organization storage area, crafts area, copy center, small meeting room, medium meeting room, three administrative offices, health center, and wireless Internet access

At Kalamazoo College, surveys of both students and faculty/staff identified a real need to renovate the Student Center. "The building was old and in need of many structural updates," said Kate Leishman, assistant director of student activities. "Reports also drew attention to the lack of noncurricular activities/social connections on campus."

Students were not only heavily involved throughout the process, but also fought for LEED certification. The renovated building achieved LEED Silver.

University of Wisconsin–Stevens Point (renovation/addition)
Dreyfus University Center
Stevens Point, Wis.

SUBMITTED BY: Susan Crotteau, Assistant Director, Operations
Four-year, public
FULL-TIME ENROLLMENT: 9,200
ORIGINALLY OPENED: November 1958
REOPENED: January 2008
AREA RENOVATED: 118,400 sq. ft.
AREA ADDED: 34,000 sq. ft.
TOTAL AREA: 181,896 sq. ft.
FLOORS: 3
ASSIGNABLE SPACE: 65%
PROJECT COST: $23.7 million
FUNDING SOURCE: 100% student fees
ARCHITECTS: SDS Architects, Inc. – Eau Claire, Wis.; Perkins+Will – Minneapolis, Minn.
FACILITIES RENOVATED: Snack bar, cafeteria, coffee shop, quiet lounge, television lounge, nightclub, patio, multicultural center, ticket office, information center, gallery, bookstore, retail space, three medium meeting rooms, two large meeting rooms, two multipurpose rooms, administrative office space, and broadened wireless Internet access
FACILITIES ADDED: Nine other food areas, patio, e-mail kiosk, retail space, copy center, guest room, three medium meeting rooms, and a theater

To serve the University of Wisconsin–Stevens Point's more than 9,000 students a day, the original Dreyfus Student Center needed an update.

"The original building was approaching 50 years of age with failing mechanical, plumbing, and electrical systems. The dining services kitchen facilities were unable to serve student needs. Overall, the facility was a very tired friend who needed an extreme makeover," said Susan Crotteau, assistant director, operations.

The new building is LEED Silver certified and features a 220-person theater and 800-person capacity ballroom.

"We have incorporated many aspects of sustainability and actively involved students in the design and operational decisions for the facility," Cratteau said. "It is truly the students' building."

Photos courtesy of University of Wisconsin–Stevens Point

124

Northern Kentucky University (new building)
Student Union
Highland Heights, Ky.

SUBMITTED BY: Sarah Aikman, Director
Four-year, public, urban, commuter
FULL-TIME ENROLLMENT: 15,000
OPENED: July 2008
TOTAL AREA: 126,030 sq. ft.
FLOORS: 3
ASSIGNABLE SPACE: 66%
PROJECT COST: $37 million
FUNDING SOURCE: 100% student fees
ARCHITECT: Omni Architects – Lexington, Ky.
FACILITIES ADDED: Starbucks, snack bar, dining room, seven other food areas, two television lounges, nightclub, three patios, 10,770-sq.-ft. student organization suite, two information centers, e-mail kiosk, two retail areas, games room, seven large meeting rooms, multipurpose rooms with three sections, 8,500-sq.-ft. administrative office space, and wireless Internet access

The existence of the new Student Union at Northern Kentucky University is owed to the efforts of students, according to Director Sarah Aikman.

In 2003, the students decided that a new union was needed. After being denied state funding, the students voted to increase student fees to make their wish a reality.

"They were willing to pay for something that they would never have the opportunity to enjoy," Aikman said. "It was something the students wanted, fought for, and made a reality."

The first campus building in the state to be entirely student fee-funded, the new Student Union is constantly busy, giving the commuter students a place to go before, after, and between classes.

"It is an incredible building, with great meeting spaces, lounge spaces, food venues, and awesome furniture," Aikman said. "It has really made Northern Kentucky University feel like a 'real' college campus."

2010

Boise State University

Castleton State College

Curry College

University of Georgia

Iowa State University

Lawrence University

University of Maryland–College Park

Minnesota State University–Mankato

University of North Carolina–Charlotte

University of North Florida

University of San Deigo

University of South Florida

Texas A&M University–Commerce

Valparaiso University

Renovation & Construction
showcase

Boise State University (renovation/addition)
Student Union
Boise, Idaho

SUBMITTED BY: Jack Rahmann, Director
Four-year, public, urban, commuter
FULL-TIME ENROLLMENT: 20,000
OPENED: Sept. 1, 1999
REOPENED: Aug. 14, 2009
AREA RENOVATED: 27,000 sq. ft.
AREA ADDED: 67,000 sq. ft.
FLOORS: 3
ASSIGNABLE SPACE: 75%
PROJECT COST: $30 million
FUNDING SOURCE: 100% student fees
ARCHITECT: MHTN – Salt Lake City; Lombard Conrad Architects – Boise, Idaho
FACILITIES RENOVATED: Snack bar, cafeteria, coffee house, two other food areas, two quiet lounges, patio, multicultural center, information center, gallery, graphics center, bookstore, retail area, bowling lane, games room, multipurpose room, and five administrative offices
FACILITIES ADDED: Six quiet lounges, 2,000-sq.-ft. student organization suite, 400-sq.-ft. student organization storage area, two e-mail kiosks, crafts center, bookstore, two small meeting rooms, two medium-sized meeting rooms, multi-purpose room, and four administrative offices

The Boise State University Student Union has seen a lot of growth since opening in 1999. During the past 10 years, student enrollment increased from 14,000 to 20,000. And daily building counts grew by 15 percent annually over the last six years to 7,000 daily. It was time for the Student Union to expand.

"The Student Union is now a 252,000-square-foot facility," said Jack Rahmann, director. "[There is a] new grand ballroom, new dining hall and kitchen, additional study lounges, and programming space."

The new design improved access to the building and incorporated sustainable elements, such as a geothermal heating, ventilation, and air conditioning system; a cardboard compactor; a grease storage system; and low-volume bathroom fixtures.

Castleton State College (renovation/addition)
Campus Center
Castleton, Vt.

SUBMITTED BY: Victoria Angis, Assistant Dean for Campus Life
Four-year, public, rural, residential
FULL-TIME ENROLLMENT: 1,995
OPENED: Aug. 25, 1975
REOPENED: Aug. 10, 2009
AREA RENOVATED: 20,308 sq. ft.
AREA ADDED: 11,453 sq. ft.
TOTAL AREA: 31,761 sq. ft.
FLOORS: 3
ASSIGNABLE SPACE: 82%
PROJECT COST: $7.5 million
FUNDING SOURCE: 68% student fees; 32% institutional funding
ARCHITECT: JMZ Architects and Planners, P.C. – Glens Falls, N.Y.
FACILITIES RENOVATED: Branded food concept, quiet lounge, patio, information center, bookstore, games room, two medium-sized meeting rooms, administrative office space, mail room, and broadened wireless Internet access
FACILITIES ADDED: Another food venue, student organization suite, student organization storage area, retail space, multipurpose room, wellness center, and four restrooms

In 1975, the Campus Center at Castleton State College was built quickly and cheaply for an on-campus residential population of 600 after a fire destroyed another building on campus that provided similar services. Years later, the center was in need of an update and expansion.

"Not only was the entire existing structure renovated inside and out, but also several key service areas were moved within the building and given more space," said Victoria Angis, assistant dean for campus life. "The new Campus Center has been part of a major transition for our campus. Students are now proud to say they go to Castleton."

The Campus Center was built to LEED Silver specifications as 75 percent of existing walls, floors, and roof were reused along with using local materials and low-VOC materials and furnishings.

Photos by Ennis Duling

Curry College (new building)
Student Center
Milton, Mass.

SUBMITTED BY: Allison Coutts, Interim Director
Four-year, private, urban, residential
FULL-TIME ENROLLMENT: 1,900
OPENED: Aug. 14, 2009
TOTAL AREA: 84,000 sq. ft.
FLOORS: 4
ASSIGNABLE SPACE: 76%
PROJECT COST: $35 million
ARCHITECT: CBT Childs, Bertman & Tseckares Inc. – Boston; LDL Studio – Providence, R.I.
FACILITIES ADDED: Snack bar, cafeteria, dining room, quiet lounge, television lounge, patio, 1,395-sq. ft. student organization suite, 800-sq.-ft. student organization storage area, information center, three e-mail kiosks, fitness room, locker room, copy center, bookstore, games room, outdoor equipment, spiritual room, two small meeting rooms, medium-sized meeting room, administrative office space, campus life offices, athletics offices, food service offices, and wireless Internet access

The Curry College Student Center was built based on two needs of the campus: increased dining capacity and cocurricular gathering space. The building was designed like a shopping mall to bring out those features and encourage student and staff engagement.

"The unique design has elements that bring students, faculty, and staff to the facility for a variety of reasons and fosters interaction … once they have arrived," said Allison Coutts, interim director. "It encourages cross connections through all constituencies of campus."

Some sustainable aspects of the design include gas-fired cooling, high-efficiency boilers and lighting, low-flow toilets and faucets, and a 300-point energy management system.

The University of Georgia (renovation/addition)
Tate Student Center
Atlanta, Ga.

SUBMITTED BY: Willie Banks, Director
Four-year, public, residential
FULL-TIME ENROLLMENT: 34,000
OPENED: Oct. 20, 1983
REOPENED: Aug. 30, 2009
AREA RENOVATED: 100,000 sq. ft.
AREA ADDED: 95,000 sq. ft.
TOTAL AREA: 195,000 sq. ft.
FLOORS: 5
ASSIGNABLE SPACE: 45%
PROJECT COST: $60.2 million
FUNDING SOURCE: 80% student fees; 20% institution funding
ARCHITECT: Cooper Carry – Atlanta; MHTN – Salt Lake City
FACILITIES RENOVATED: Patio, student organization offices, student organization storage area, ticket office, six e-mail kiosks, gallery, two medium-sized meeting rooms, theater, administrative office space, and dance rehearsal space
FACILITIES ADDED: Three branded food concepts, faculty club, quiet lounge, television lounge, information center, one ticket office, eight e-mail kiosks, copy center, spiritual room, four medium-sized meeting rooms, three large meeting rooms, multipurpose room, and wireless Internet access

When it originally opened in 1983, the Tate Student Center was just Phase 1 of a two-phase project to bring a first-rate union to the University of Georgia campus. However, budgetary concerns made it so the second phase was never added—until now.

"This project was an amazing journey for our students and staff," said Willie Banks, director. "During the 18 months of construction, services were provided without interruption."

The project brought together different departments and students across campus, and it is the university's first LEED-certified building, earning a LEED Silver rating.

"There were many challenges for this project," Banks said. "But the team of architects, contractors, students, and staff ultimately produced a top-rate union for the university community."

Photos by Don Reagin

Iowa State University (renovation/addition)
Memorial Union
Ames, Iowa

SUBMITTED BY: Richard Reynolds, Director
Four-year, public, residential
FULL-TIME ENROLLMENT: 27,945
OPENED: April 16, 2009
AREA RENOVATED: 42,232 sq. ft.
AREA ADDED: 35,684 sq. ft.
TOTAL AREA: 318,673 sq. ft.
FLOORS: 8
ASSIGNABLE SPACE: 75%
PROJECT COST: $22.9 million
FUNDING SOURCE: 61% student fees; 28% bookstore funding; 8% private donations; 3% institutional funding
ARCHITECT: HLKB Architecture – Des Moines, Iowa
FACILITIES RENOVATED: Branded food area, snack bar, quiet lounge, patio, multicultural center, information center, 25 e-mail kiosks, copy center, bookstore, medium-sized meeting room, and multipurpose room
FACILITIES ADDED: Patio, bookstore, administrative office space, and wireless Internet access

Between 1928, when the Memorial Union was originally built, and 1977, it underwent 10 additions. And in 1996, another addition allowed for the renovation of a food court and student organization office space. But the building was still in need of work; so, in 2003, students approved a fee to fund another renovation/addition project.

"Spaces in the original building were restored rather than renovated," said Richard Reynolds, director. "Artisans were contracted to restore the façade of the building and replicate architectural details in the ballroom and lobby area."

This student-led initiative resulted in an updated Memorial Union that strives to blend the new and old.

133

Lawrence University (new building)
Richard and Margot Warch Campus Center
Appleton, Wis.

SUBMITTED BY: Gregory Griffin, Director
Four-year, private, residential
FULL-TIME ENROLLMENT: 14,000
OPENED: Sept. 18, 2009
TOTAL AREA: 107,000 sq. ft.
FLOORS: 5
ASSIGNABLE SPACE: 60%
PROJECT COST: $35 million
FUNDING SOURCE: 100% private donations
ARCHITECT: Uihlein-Wilson Architects, Inc. – Milwaukee, Wis.; KSS Architects – Princeton, N.J.
FACILITIES ADDED: Snack bar, cafeteria, coffee house, three dining rooms, two quiet lounges, television lounge, three patios, 944-sq.-ft. student organization office suite, 800-sq.-ft. student organization storage area, information center, three e-mail kiosks, ticket office, gallery, two retail spaces, two small meeting rooms, one medium-sized meeting room, theater, two multipurpose rooms, administrative office space, and broadened wireless Internet access

The Task Force on Residential Life at Lawrence University found that the campus's original union was not meeting students' needs. They wanted a facility that better complimented residential life and supported the institution's educational mission. Director Gregory Griffin believes the Warch Campus Center addresses these issues.

"The Campus Center represents the culmination of more than two decades of planning and aspiration and represents a monumental step forward in the development of the residential campus setting of the university," he said. "It is truly a transformational building."

The Campus Center is LEED Gold certified; natural materials were used during construction and some sustainable features include a green roof, water-efficient toilet fixtures, and native landscaping.

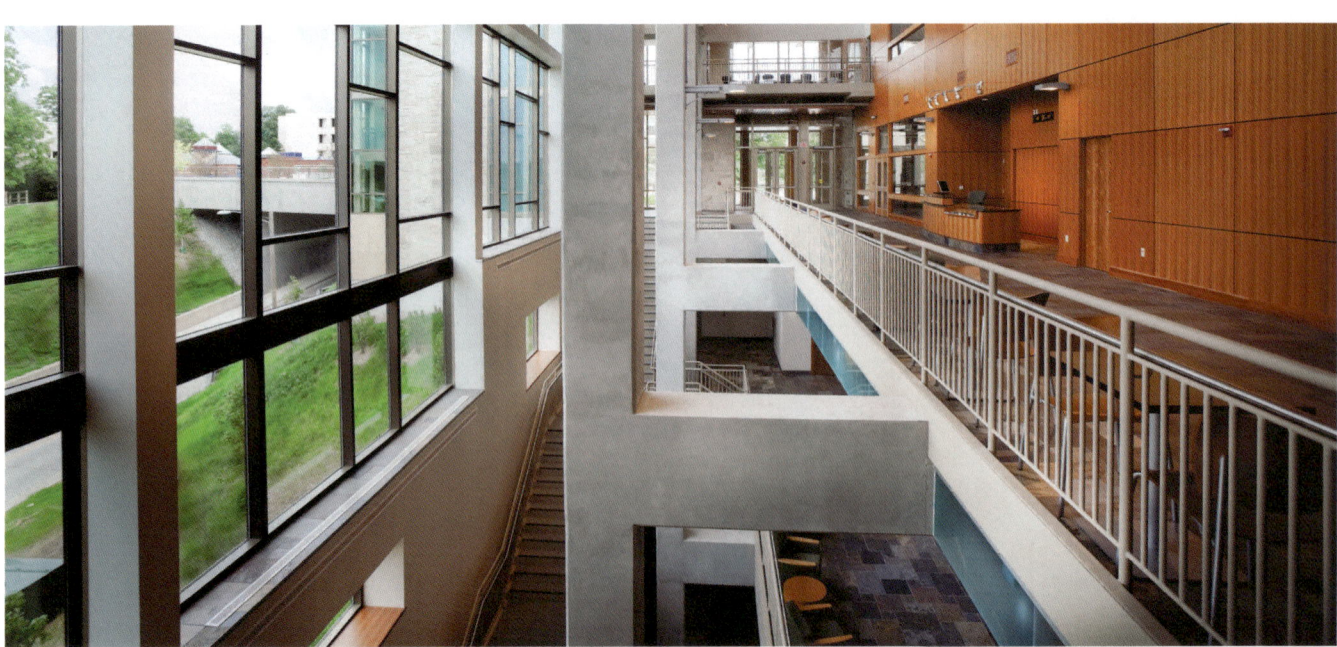

University of Maryland–College Park (renovation)
Stamp Student Union
College Park, Md.

SUBMITTED BY: Stephen Gnadt, Associate Director
Four-year, public, urban
FULL-TIME ENROLLMENT: 35,000
OPENED: July 1, 1986
REOPENED: Nov. 15, 2009
AREA RENOVATED: 5,200 sq. ft.
TOTAL AREA: 286,092 sq. ft.
FLOORS: 5
ASSIGNABLE SPACE: 60%
PROJECT COST: $2.3 million
FUNDING SOURCE: 60% student fees;
   40% generated revenue
ARCHITECT: Murphy & Dittenhafer – Baltimore
FACILITIES RENOVATED: Two multipurpose rooms

In previous decades, two outdoor courtyard spaces around the University of Maryland–College Park's Stamp Student Union had been enclosed with glass roofing structures. However, these roofs caused ongoing problems with leaking, and the direct sunlight from the skylights prevented the rooms from being used for multimedia presentations.

To address these problems, the rooms were completely renovated to include windows that filter in natural, but not direct, sunlight; new flooring; and a green roof to help deal with previous water issues. Overall, the rooms are much more energy-efficient.

"This small renovation project transformed a problem space into an environmentally friendly and sustainable space that the entire campus wants to use," said Stephen Gnadt, associate director. "It shows how sustainable practices can solve typical building renovation problems."

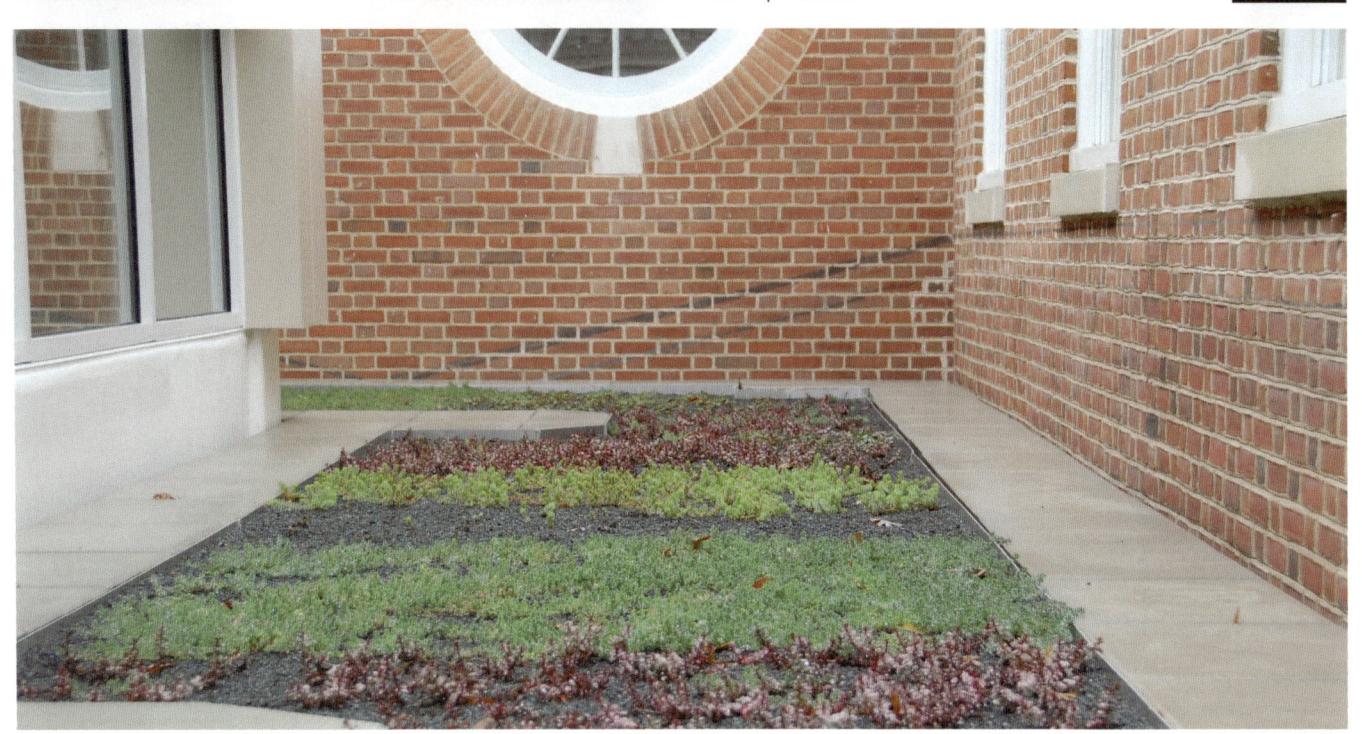

Photos by Stephen Gnadt

Minnesota State University–Mankato
The Ostrander
Mankato, Minn. (renovation)

SUBMITTED BY: Laurie Woodward, Director
Four-year, public, rural, commuter, residential
FULL-TIME ENROLLMENT: 14,000
OPENED: Oct. 2, 1972
REOPENED: Oct. 7, 2009
TOTAL AREA: 7,000 sq. ft.
FLOORS: 2
ASSIGNABLE SPACE: 62%
PROJECT COST: $1.6 million
FUNDING SOURCE: 100% student fees
ARCHITECT: R.L. Engerbretson – Mankato, Minn.
FACILITIES RENOVATED: A theater and broadened wireless Internet access

A maintenance study showed that the Ostrander Auditorium, located on the first floor of Minnesota State University's Centennial Student Union, was in need of repair in many areas. The auditorium was stripped to its shell and completely rebuilt, receiving new seating, a stage, curtains, and a heating, ventilation, and cooling system.

"The Ostrander is the first place that students visit on campus," said Laurie Woodward, director. "And now, the facility provides a great first impression."

The lighting and sound systems as well as HVAC system are all energy-efficient, and new technology was incorporated in the design.

University of North Carolina–Charlotte (new building)
Student Union
Charlotte, N.C.

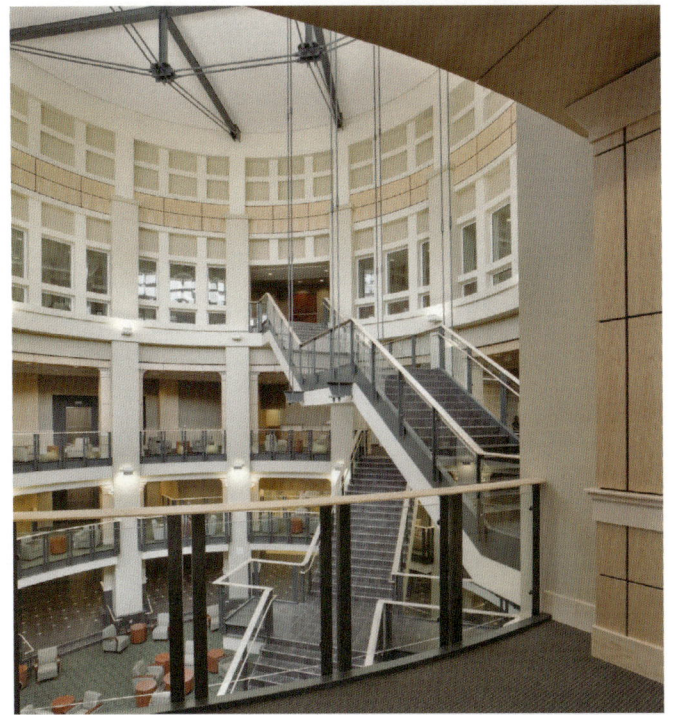

SUBMITTED BY: Jerry Mann, Executive Director
Four-year, public, urban, residential
FULL-TIME ENROLLMENT: 24,700
OPENED: July 15, 2009
TOTAL AREA: 196,000 sq. ft.
FLOORS: 4
ASSIGNABLE SPACE: 65%
PROJECT COST: $59.9 million
FUNDING SOURCE: 94% student fees; 6% university auxiliary unit
ARCHITECT: FWA Group – Charlotte, N.C.
FACILITIES ADDED: Five branded food concepts, cafeteria, other food area, quiet lounge, television lounge, five patios, 6,858-sq.-ft. student organization suite, 516-sq.-ft. student organization storage area, information center, e-mail kiosk, gallery, copy center, bookstore, four retail spaces, seven small meeting rooms, six medium-sized meeting rooms, one large meeting room, theater, multipurpose room with nine sections, administrative office space, six other lounges, student media area, leadership area, and wireless Internet access

The existing union at the University of North Carolina–Charlotte was inadequate. It was determined that the cost of a renovation would not allow for a suitable facility, so the decision was made to start from scratch and build a new union.

"The new building offers an efficient, open design that invites interaction and creates the living room feel that makes for a successful union," said Jerry Mann, executive director. "It is a building that has done what every good union should do—include the right combination of dining, retail, lounge, meeting, and event space to create a gathering point for all members of campus to find community."

The Student Union is designed to achieve LEED certification; it has waterless urinals, a white roof, charging area for electric vehicles, and occupancy sensors. Sustainable practices also were used throughout the construction.

University of North Florida (new building)
Student Union
Jacksonville, Fla.

SUBMITTED BY: Justin Camputaro, Director
Four-year, public, rural, residential
FULL-TIME ENROLLMENT: 15,430
OPENED: April 10, 2009
TOTAL AREA: 157,415 sq. ft.
FLOORS: 3
ASSIGNABLE SPACE: 73%
PROJECT COST: $50.4 million
FUNDING SOURCE: 52% student fees; 39% institutional funding; 8% government; 1% private donations
ARCHITECT: Rink Design Partnership, Inc. – Jacksonville, Fla.
FACILITIES ADDED: Four branded food concepts, snack bar, pub, dining room, two television lounges, five patios, multicultural center, 10,794-sq. ft. student organization suite, 1,956-sq. ft. student organization storage area, two information centers, four e-mail kiosks, gallery, copy center, bookstore, retail area, games room, spiritual room, four small meeting rooms, medium-sized meeting rooms, three large meeting rooms, theater, multipurpose room with four sections, administrative offices, graduate student lounge, outdoor amphitheater, and wireless Internet access

Though opened in 1972, the University of North Florida never had a true union. A campus facility called the Robinson Student Life Center acted as a union but was unable to offer all the amenities that students desired. Therefore, in 2000, the student government decided that the construction of a union was a priority.

"The Student Union has brought so much to our campus," said Justin Camputaro, director. "It is not only a recruitment tool we never had, but also it is a retention tool. It is the new 'home' for the students, and they are very happy for it."

The university is finalizing the LEED certification process, and staff members believe the new building is likely to reach at least LEED Silver, partially because of the waterless urinals, use of reclaimed water, and use of recycled and local materials in the construction process.

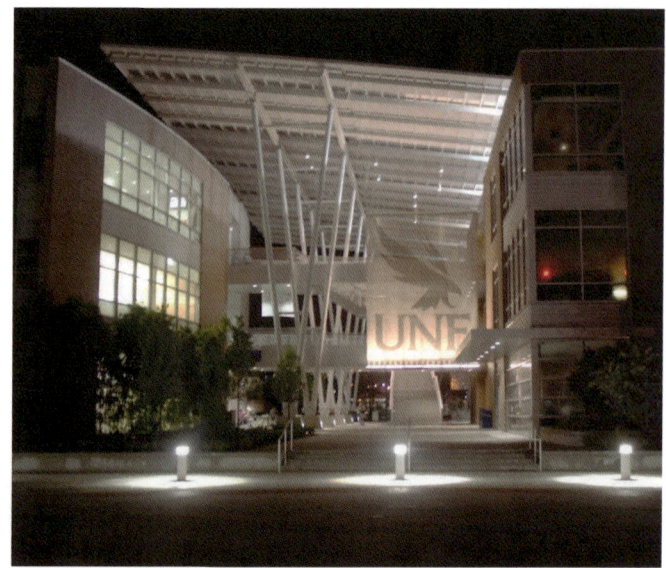

Photos by Severine Wider

138

University of San Diego (renovation/addition)
Student Life Pavilion
San Diego, Calif.

SUBMITTED BY: Kathy McIntosh, Student Life Initiatives Project Manager
Four-year, private, urban, residential
FULL-TIME ENROLLMENT: 7,200
OPENED: July 1, 1986
REOPENED: Nov. 15, 2009
AREA RENOVATED: 13,790 sq. ft.
AREA ADDED: 53,025 sq. ft.
TOTAL AREA: 129,025 sq. ft.
FLOORS: 5
ASSIGNABLE SPACE: 90%
PROJECT COST: $42.5 million
FUNDING SOURCE: 34% private donations; 33% student fees; 33% institutional funding
ARCHITECT: Hamm and Goldman Architects – New York City; Mosher Drew Watson Ferguson – San Diego
FACILITIES RENOVATED: Dining room, faculty club, other food area, information center, outdoor equipment, small meeting room, multipurpose room, and administrative office space
FACILITIES ADDED: Snack bar, cafeteria, pub, other food area, quiet lounge, three television lounges, three patios, multicultural center, 1,400-sq.-ft. student organization suite, 500-sq.-ft. student organization storage area, information center, e-mail kiosk, gallery, locker room, graphics shop, two retail spaces, games room, outdoor equipment, three small meeting rooms, multipurpose room, administrative office space, and wireless Internet access

The Student Life Pavilion was built to meet the technological and involvement needs of University of San Diego students.

"It was designed to provide large, open spaces where students can interact with one another, significantly expanded hours, dining options that reflect students' palates, work spaces for organizations, and a marketplace," said Kathy McIntosh, student life initiatives project manager.

The university is planning to seek LEED Gold certification. The building features many sustainable aspects, such as a food decomposition unit, windows that are able to be opened and used to regulate temperature, and a green roof.

University of South Florida (new building)
Marshall Student Center
Tampa, Fla.

SUBMITTED BY: Joe Synovec, Director
Four-year, public, urban
FULL-TIME ENROLLMENT: 39,852
OPENED: April 15, 2009
TOTAL AREA: 305,571 sq. ft.
FLOORS: 4
ASSIGNABLE SPACE: 76%
PROJECT COST: $65 million
FUNDING SOURCE: 100% student fees
ARCHITECT: Gould Evans Associates – Tampa, Fla.; Sasaki Associates, Inc. – Watertown, Mass.
FACILITIES ADDED: Six branded food concepts, two snack bars, pub, coffee house, another food area, five quiet lounges, two television lounges, two patios, multicultural center, 5,289-sq.-ft. student organization suite, information center, ticket office, gallery, seven retail spaces, games room, three small meeting rooms, 12 medium-sized meeting rooms, five large meeting rooms, two theaters, seven multipurpose rooms, student life tower with four floors, and wireless Internet access

The original Marshall Center was created to serve the University of South Florida when it first opened with an enrollment of 2,500 students. Today, more than 39,000 students are enrolled at the university, and they needed a union that fit their increased population.

"The Marshall Student Center is having a significant impact on student life," said Joe Synovec, director. "Much more than the original Student Center, there has been an amazing transformation in the role that it plays on campus. It is playing a vital role in student recruiting, retention, and development like never before."

Sustainability was a consideration during the building process; recycling was done on site, and the building incorporates recycled materials for the flooring and ceiling tiles.

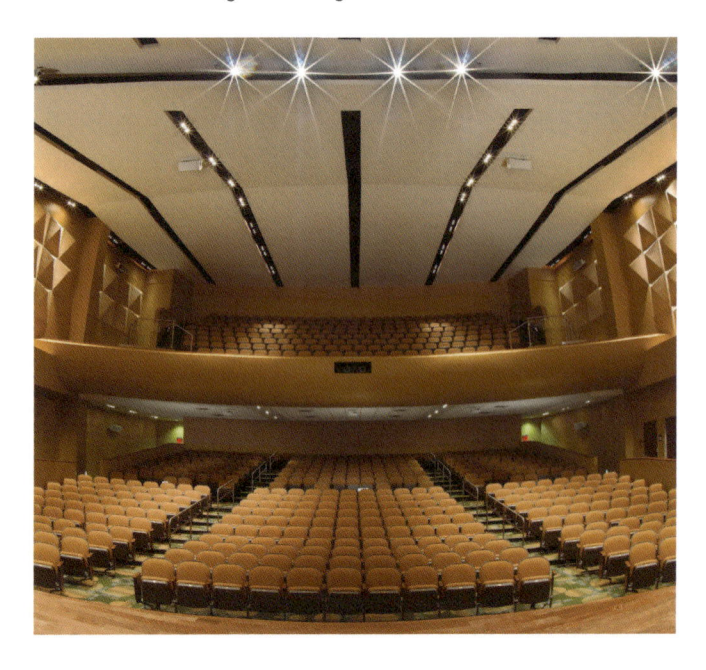

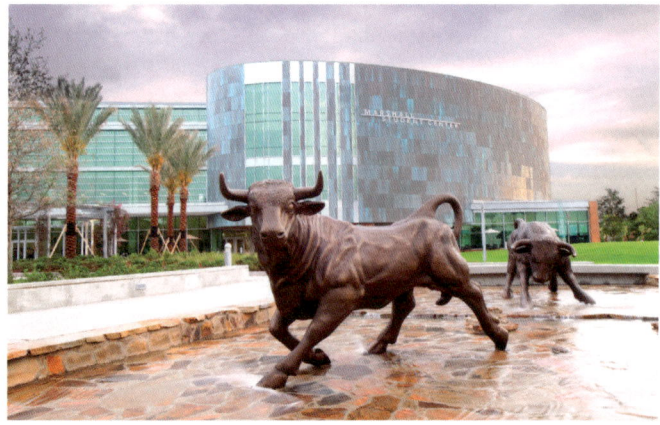

Photos by Armstrong Ceilings

Texas A&M University–Commerce (new building)
Sam Rayburn Student Center
Commerce, Texas

SUBMITTED BY: Rick Miller, Director
Four-year, public, rural, residential
FULL-TIME ENROLLMENT: 9,600
OPENED: Jan. 30, 2009
TOTAL AREA: 95,083 sq. ft.
FLOORS: 2
ASSIGNABLE SPACE: 68%
PROJECT COST: $20.8 million
FUNDING SOURCE: 68% student fees; 32% institutional funding
ARCHITECT: WTW Architects – Pittsburgh; GideonToal – Fort Worth, Texas
FACILITIES ADDED: Three branded food concepts, cafeteria, other food area, four quiet lounges, nightclub, two patios, 5,005-sq.-ft student organization suite, 977-sq.-ft. student organization storage area, information center, two locker rooms, graphics shop, copy center, bookstore, two retail spaces, games room, small meeting room, two medium-sized meeting rooms, five large meeting rooms, multipurpose room with three sections, administrative office space, five auxiliary/food service areas, identification card office, and wireless Internet access

Feasibility studies showed that not only was the original union facility at Texas A&M University–Commerce in need of an update, but also a renovation would not meet the campus community's needs. It was decided that a new building was necessary.

"The Sam Rayburn Student Center has many features that make it an easy-to-use, elegant, and practical facility," said Rick Miller, director. "The project was done with a modest budget to provide a building that is student-centered. While the building is modern, the tradition of 'The Union' lives on in this amazing gift the students have provided the campus. It has truly become a laboratory for learning and service."

LEED best practices were used during the construction of the new union. Materials, design, and use of technology aid in conserving energy and utility usage.

Valparaiso University
Harre Union (new building)
Valparaiso, Ind.

SUBMITTED BY: Larry Mosher, Director
Four-year, private, residential
FULL-TIME ENROLLMENT: 4,000
OPENED: Jan. 4, 2009
TOTAL AREA: 202,000 sq. ft.
FLOORS: 3
ASSIGNABLE SPACE: 88%
PROJECT COST: $74 million
FUNDING SOURCE: 100% private donations
ARCHITECT: Sasaki and Associates – Boston; Design Organization – Valparaiso, Ind.
FACILITIES ADDED: Branded food concept, snack bar, cafeteria, quiet lounge, three patios, multicultural center, 5,000-sq.-ft. student organization suite, 900-sq.-ft. student organization storage area, information center, ticket office, eight e-mail kiosks, two locker rooms, graphics shop, book store, games room, outdoor equipment, two small meeting rooms, three medium-sized meeting rooms, two large meeting rooms, multipurpose room with three sections, administrative office space, career center, international/multicultural programs area, integrated marketing, and wireless Internet access

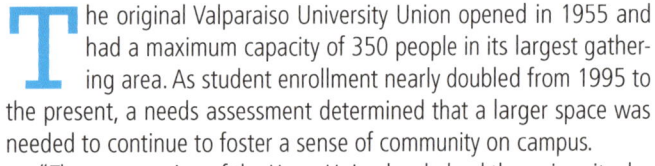

The original Valparaiso University Union opened in 1955 and had a maximum capacity of 350 people in its largest gathering area. As student enrollment nearly doubled from 1995 to the present, a needs assessment determined that a larger space was needed to continue to foster a sense of community on campus.

"The construction of the Harre Union has helped the university develop a true sense of community by completing the heart of campus," said Larry Mosher, director. "It has become the true crossroads of the campus. It is a place where community can come collaborate, debate, compromise, and celebrate."

Additionally, the building includes green features, such as a cooking oil collection system and occupancy sensors that control lighting and temperature. According to Mosher, the Harre Union was built to LEED Silver standards though the university is not seeking certification.

Photos by Aimee Tomasek and Arah Kessler

2011

Clarkson University
University of Alabama
Armstrong Atlantic State University
Ball State University
University of Colorado
California State University–Channel Islands
California State University–Sacramento
University of Memphis
University of Missouri–Columbia
University of Missouri–Kansas City
The Ohio State University
Old Dominion University
University of Rochester
University of Southern California
State University of New York–New Paltz
Vanderbilt University
Winthrop University
University of Wisconsin–Superior
College of Wooster

Renovation & Construction
showcase

The building that housed the Cheel Campus Center was originally constructed as Clarkson University's hockey arena, with which it shared space. When students started to see a need for a space dedicated solely to student life, they lobbied the university president and board of trustees to build a new union. Students even agreed to double the activities fee to pay for construction and continued support of the new building.

Efforts by Clarkson University students worked. On Aug. 23, 2010, the new Student Center was opened. It not only helped build community on campus, but also the building itself is a great addition to campus. One design feature that Associate Dean of Students Jason Enser believes stands out above the rest is the Forum space.

"Architecturally, the Forum space is designed around an Adirondack-style roofline with a glass wall opening to the central green space on campus. It has a grand stairway large enough for students to sit on going all the way from the top floor to the bottom floor," he said. "The building is aesthetically stunning and has revitalized life on campus."

SUBMITTED BY: Jason Enser, Associate Dean of Students
FOUR-YEAR, PRIVATE, RURAL, RESIDENTIAL
FULL-TIME ENROLLMENT: 3,000
OPENED: Aug. 23, 2010
AREA: 57,000 sq. ft.
FLOORS: 3
ASSIGNABLE SPACE: 75%
PROJECT COST: $25 million
FUNDING SOURCE: 67% private donations; 33% student fees
ARCHITECT: Perkins+Will – Boston
FACILITIES ADDED: Snack bar, cafeteria, pub, coffee house, quiet lounge, television lounge, multicultural center, six student organization areas, 5,000-sq.-ft. student organization suite, two student organization storage areas, information center, locker room, retail space, two games rooms, spiritual center, two small meeting rooms, theater, multipurpose room with three sections, administrative office space, and wireless Internet access

Clarkson University (new building)
Student Center
Potsdam, N.Y.

University of Alabama (renovation)
Ferguson Student Center
Tuscaloosa, Ala.

SUBMITTED BY: April Sanders, Assistant Manager, Facilities Operations
FOUR-YEAR, PUBLIC
FULL-TIME ENROLLMENT: 30,232
OPENED: 1971
REOPENED: May 14, 2010
AREA RENOVATED: 8,326 sq. ft.
FLOORS: 3
ASSIGNABLE SPACE: 34%
PROJECT COST: $386,076
FUNDING SOURCE: 100% private and institutional funding
ARCHITECT: Turner Batson – Birmingham, Ala.
FACILITIES RENOVATED: Student organization suite and student organization storage area

Since it was originally built, the number of student organizations at the University of Alabama's Ferguson Student Center has grown. More than 250 groups call the union home. Therefore, it was a necessity to revamp the student organization space to meet the needs of all groups.

"The SOURCE is a physical space for all registered student organizations on campus," Assistant Manager, Facilities Operations April Sanders said. "This open space provides printing, faxing, copying, computer use, meeting space with a flat-screen television for presentations, bulletin board supplies, event supplies, application pick up/drop off, and other services for registered student organizations."

Additionally, the Warner O. Moore Hall of Fame recognizes outstanding contributions to student life, Sanders said.

Armstrong Atlantic State University (new building)
Student Union
Savannah, Ga.

SUBMITTED BY: Chris Nowicki, Assistant Director, Student Union and Activities
FOUR-YEAR, RESIDENTIAL, PUBLIC
FULL-TIME ENROLLMENT: 7,682
OPENED: June 15, 2010
TOTAL AREA: 60,000 sq. ft.
FLOORS: 2
ASSIGNABLE SPACE: 75%
PROJECT COST: $20 million
FUNDING SOURCE: 100% student fees
ARCHITECT: Burt Hill – Philadelphia
FACILITIES ADDED: Cafeteria, coffee house, dining room, three television lounges, two patios, two student organization spaces, five student organization suites, two student organization storage areas, two e-mail kiosks, bookstore, retail space, three small meeting rooms, two medium meeting rooms, theater, multipurpose room with three sections, administrative office space, and broadened wireless Internet access

During the last five years, Armstrong Atlantic State University has made the transition from a commuter campus to a residential campus, seeing an enrollment increase and a need for a place for "students to interact with other students," said Student Union and Activities Assistant Director Chris Nowicki. And so, plans began to build the Student Union.

Students were involved with the building from the beginning, offering design suggestions, helping to choose furniture, and going on site visits to other institutions to see a union in action.

"The large involvement of the student body in this process truly makes the building the students' building," Nowicki said. "The Armstrong Student Union has truly brought the campus together."

The Student Union offers the campus multiple programming areas, including an outdoor performance stage and large grass areas. As the university's first green building, the union also has many sustainable features. A ceramic cooling tower reduces air conditioning costs, 75 percent of the building's interior is exposed to natural light, and a reflective roofing membrane reduces solar heat in the building.

Photos by Richard Johnson

Ball State University (renovation)
L.A. Pittenger Student Center
Muncie, Ind.

SUBMITTED BY: Bruce Morgan, Director, Student Center and Programs
FOUR-YEAR, PUBLIC, RESIDENTIAL
FULL-TIME ENROLLMENT: 19,965
OPENED: 1952
REOPENED: February 2010
TOTAL AREA: 180,500 sq. ft.
AREA RENOVATED: 135,000 sq. ft.
FLOORS: 4
ASSIGNABLE SPACE: 68%
PROJECT COST: $20.5 million
FUNDING SOURCE: 100% internal revenues
ARCHITECT: The Estopinal Group – Jeffersonville, Ind.
FACILITIES RENOVATED: Snack bar, cafeteria, quiet lounge, television lounge, two patios, five student organization areas, information center, e-mail kiosk, games room, three small meeting rooms, eight medium meeting rooms, five large meeting rooms, two multipurpose rooms, post office, and five lounges
FACILITIES ADDED: Two branded food concepts, television lounge, and two small meeting rooms

The L.A. Pittenger Student Center at Ball State University was in need of an upgrade.

"The infrastructure needed to be replaced and asbestos needed to be removed," Director of the Student Center and Programs Bruce Morgan said. "The main entrance to the building was not inviting. The dining room had a low ceiling, no natural light, and the design and finishes were outdated."

Students filled out surveys, student leaders toured other unions across the United States, and focus groups helped determine how to serve different demographics.

"Our renovation exemplifies how involving students early in the planning process, listening to their needs, and responding can ensure the success of a major renovation," Morgan said.

The entrance now invites people to the building. The dining room is two stories and full of natural light. Student organizations were moved to a prime location in the building. All meeting rooms have state-of-the-art technology. Additionally, all new buildings at Ball State must achieve at least LEED Silver certification. Thus, new energy efficient equipment was installed, sustainable finishes were selected, and products that create a smaller environmental footprint were used.

"Our goal was to provide a better environment within this facility for the occupants, to improve the overall building efficiency, and to create a long-term, better performing building," Morgan said. "And we feel we have successfully obtained those goals."

University of Colorado (renovation)
University Memorial Center
Boulder, Colo.

SUBMITTED BY: Carlos Garcia, Director
FOUR-YEAR, PUBLIC, RESIDENTIAL
FULL-TIME ENROLLMENT: 30,000
OPENED: 1953
REOPENED: Oct. 15, 2010
AREA RENOVATED: 16,322 sq. ft.
FLOORS: 1
ASSIGNABLE SPACE: 100%
PROJECT COST: $2 million
FUNDING SOURCE: 70% student fees; 30% self-funded and future revenues
ARCHITECT: OZ Architecture – Boulder, Colo.; Porter Khouw Consulting – Crofton, Md.
FACILITIES RENOVATED: Cafeteria

The Alferd Packer Grill and Dining Rooms at the University of Colorado's Memorial Center had not been renovated since 1986, and it was starting to show.

"The renovation opened up the area, improved traffic flow, and provided more flexibility for future changes," said Director Carlos Garcia. "The newly renovated area provides more options for food choices and accessibility for students, faculty, and staff."

The renovation qualified as a LEED-certified project as at least half of the construction waste was recycled, products used contained at least 10 percent recycled materials, and indoor air quality was maintained by using low-emitting paint and other products.

"Increased efficiency, sustainability, and flexibility make the Alferd Packer Grill the University Memorial Center's new pride," Garcia said.

Photos by Jale Claeys and Anne Robertson

California State University–Channel Islands (renovation/addition)
Student Union
Camarillo, Calif.

SUBMITTED BY: Genevieve Evans Taylor, ASI Executive Director
FOUR-YEAR, PUBLIC, RURAL, RESIDENTIAL
FULL-TIME ENROLLMENT: 3,800
OPENED: March 10, 2010
TOTAL AREA: 25,100 sq. ft.
AREA ADDED: 15,500 sq. ft.
FLOORS: 2
ASSIGNABLE SPACE: 84%
PROJECT COST: $13 million
FUNDING SOURCE: 100% student fees
ARCHITECT: DLR Group/WWCOT – Santa Monica, Calif.
FACILITIES RENOVATED/ADDED: Snack bar, coffee house, two food services, two quiet lounges, television lounge, patio, 40 student organization areas, five student organization suites, two student organization storage areas, information center, e-mail kiosk, games room, two small meeting rooms, medium meeting room, multi-purpose room, administrative office space, and wireless Internet access

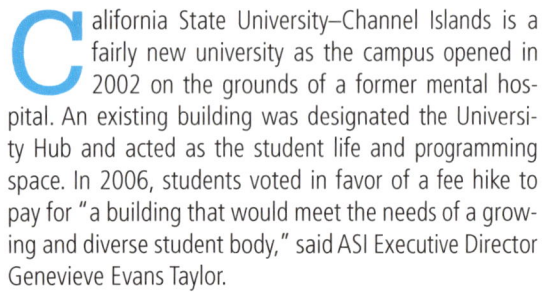

California State University–Channel Islands is a fairly new university as the campus opened in 2002 on the grounds of a former mental hospital. An existing building was designated the University Hub and acted as the student life and programming space. In 2006, students voted in favor of a fee hike to pay for "a building that would meet the needs of a growing and diverse student body," said ASI Executive Director Genevieve Evans Taylor.

Plans were made for the union to reside in the center of campus. A preexisting building was partially demolished and partially renovated. A new building was constructed next to and connected to the renovated space to create the new Student Union.

Sustainability was a "high priority" during the construction.

"The most sustainable feature is the adaptive reuse of a large portion of an existing structure, extending the life of resources used in its initial construction," Taylor said. "This is augmented by retention of mature trees, minimized footprint, and efficient structural, mechanical, and lighting systems."

Photos by Andrew Hall

California State University–Sacramento
The WELL: Recreation and Wellness Center (new building)
Sacramento, Calif.

Photos by Cesar Rubio

SUBMITTED BY: Leslie Davis, Executive Director
FOUR-YEAR, PUBLIC, URBAN, COMMUTER
FULL-TIME ENROLLMENT: 22,000
OPENED: Sept. 2, 2010
TOTAL AREA: 151,000 sq. ft.
FLOORS: 2
ASSIGNABLE SPACE: 87%
PROJECT COST: $710,000
FUNDING SOURCE: 100% student fees
ARCHITECT: Hornberger + Worstell – San Francisco; Ellerbe Becket – San Francisco
FACILITIES ADDED: Snack bar, quiet lounge, three patios, three information centers, three fitness rooms, three locker rooms, child care center, retail space, outdoor equipment, four medium meeting rooms, administrative office space, student health center, climbing wall and boulder, gym courts, racquetball courts, Mac court, and wireless Internet access

At California State University–Sacramento, those students not actively involved in varsity or intramural sports had difficulty finding a place to work out on campus. The answer: The WELL, a new recreation and wellness center that offers whole-health care services for the entire campus community. From cardio to physical therapy and a pharmacy to mental health services, the WELL is a one-stop shop.

"Unlike other campus fitness facilities that focus on exercise alone, the WELL is the new heart of Sacramento State student life, uniting fitness, medical care, and social activity spaces under one roof," said Executive Director Leslie Davis. "The combination of these vital aspects of student life will form a synergy in that the success of one will directly benefit the others."

Students have been a driving force since the beginning, voting in favor of a $110 per semester fee increase and sitting on committees to review design and offer input on the WELL.

The WELL also meets LEED Gold standards. FSC-certified wood and recycled materials were used in construction along with implementing a landfill diversion program.

"One of the WELL's most visible sustainable features is an entrance atrium with a skylight made of an innovative thermo plastic material developed by NASA that not only helps regulate building temperature, but also makes students feel welcome by bathing the space in natural light," Davis said.

University of Memphis (new building)
University Center
Memphis, Tenn.

SUBMITTED BY: Bob Barnett, Director, University Center & Michael D. Rose Theatre
FOUR-YEAR, PUBLIC, URBAN
FULL-TIME ENROLLMENT: 17,451
OPENED: Feb. 18, 2010
TOTAL AREA: 189,000 sq. ft.
FLOORS: 3
ASSIGNABLE SPACE: 93%
PROJECT COST: $53.5 million
FUNDING SOURCE: 93% student fees; 7% food service contractor investment
ARCHITECT: Haizlip Studio – Memphis, Tenn.; Fisher & Arnold – Memphis, Tenn.
FACILITIES ADDED: Three branded food concepts, four other food service areas, quiet lounge, three patios, multicultural center, four student organization suites, three student organization storage areas, information center, ticket office, e-mail kiosk, copy center, seven small meeting rooms, three large meetings rooms, six multipurpose rooms, administrative office space, senate chamber, and wireless Internet access

Originally, the University of Memphis planned to renovate its old union, built in 1968. However, the extent of the overhaul would cost more than $20 million, and the campus would still be using a dated facility. It was decided that a new building should be constructed.

"Students were part of every stage, beginning with the programming, through the finance feasibility, and on through the design/build process," Director Bob Barnett said.

Two key features of the new union are the Burger King Whopper Bar, which is the first of its kind on a college campus, as well as an 80-station computer lab that is open to the campus 24 hours a day.

"The new University Center at the University of Memphis is the largest capital project in the history of the university, is architecturally significant, and is now one of the finest student unions in the mid-south region," Barnett said.

University of Missouri–Columbia (renovation/addition)
MU Student Center
Columbia, Mo.

SUBMITTED BY: Joe Hayes, Assistant Director
FOUR-YEAR, PUBLIC, RESIDENTIAL
FULL-TIME ENROLLMENT: 32,415
OPENED: 1963
REOPENED: 2010
TOTAL AREA: 233,011 sq. ft.
AREA ADDED: 110,847 sq. ft.
AREA RENOVATED: 122,164 sq. ft.
FLOORS: 3
ASSIGNABLE SPACE: 70%
PROJECT COST: $65 million
FUNDING SOURCE: 50% student fees, 50% institutional funding
ARCHITECT: Mackey Mitchell – St. Louis; Holzman Moss Bottino – New York
FACILITIES RENOVATED: Four branded food concepts, multicultural center, student organization suite, student organization storage area, ticket office, graphics center, copy center, bookstore, retail space, games room, two small meeting rooms, medium meeting room, administrative office space, and bank
FACILITIES ADDED: Two branded food concepts, five quiet lounges, nightclub, patio, information center, two medium meeting rooms, large meeting room, four study rooms, student entrepreneurial space, and wireless Internet access

The University of Missouri's original union, the Brady Commons, opened in 1963, serving a student population of around 15,000. As enrollment grew, a few renovations and expansions to the building tried to accommodate the needs of the larger student body.

"With 10,000 students passing through Brady Commons each day, the building lacked adequate space for the growing student population to eat, study, hold meetings, and host student clubs and organizations," said Assistant Director Joe Hayes.

A complete overhaul of and addition to the current building resulted in the MU Student Center, which offers more than double the amount of useable space for students. Two special features of the union include a Leadership Lounge that displays the names of student leaders since the university's founding and Mort's Grill, which was named for alumnus Mort Walker, the creator of the Beetle Bailey comic strip.

"Our goal was to create a student center that uniquely reflected the history and spirit of our flagship campus, and we believe that we have been successful in this endeavor," Hayes said.

Sustainable features included in the construction were the use of furnishings and carpeting approved by the U.S. Green Council, incorporation of trayless dining venues, and introduction of a green cleaning program, among others.

University of Missouri-Kansas City (new building)
Student Union
Kansas City, Mo.

SUBMITTED BY: Jody Jeffries, Director
FOUR-YEAR, PUBLIC, URBAN
FULL-TIME ENROLLMENT: 11,047
OPENED: Aug. 23, 2010
TOTAL AREA: 110,000 sq. ft.
FLOORS: 5
ASSIGNABLE SPACE: 85%
PROJECT COST: $38.3 million
FUNDING SOURCE: 96% student fees; 3% private donations; 1% institutional funding
ARCHITECT: Gould Evans Associates – Kansas City, Mo.
FACILITIES ADDED: Three branded food concepts, coffee house, one other food service area, six quiet lounges, four television lounges, four patios, multicultural center, student organization suite, student organization storage area, information center, e-mail kiosk, locker room, bookstore, two medium meeting rooms, two large meeting rooms, theater, multipurpose room with four sections, administrative office space, student involvement/multicultural student affairs center, student government chamber, garden roof terrace, and wireless Internet access

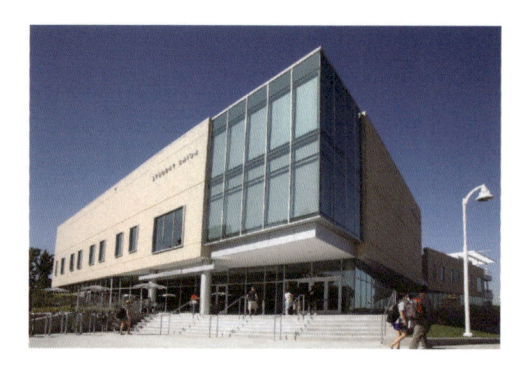

The University Center was built in 1959 at the University of Missouri–Kansas City to serve 336 on-campus residents and a small population of commuter students. Today, the university has more than 1,500 students living on campus and the overall enrollment has tripled since 1959.

"The previous facility became both antiquated in meeting student engagement needs and eventually too small to accommodate the growing vibrancy of the campus," Director Jody Jeffries said. "Student leaders had two clear expectations for the project: for occupancy to occur as quickly as possible and for the facility to be LEED certified as a minimum. Students immediately engaged in focus groups and planning teams and were involved throughout the process of program planning through construction completion."

The new Student Union achieved LEED Gold certification. Sustainable design features include: open construction and use of daylighting; energy efficient lighting and water flow restriction; use of reclaimed wood; a green roof and storm water management; food composting program; and use of regional materials, among others.

"With the accelerated growth in residential students at Kansas City's dynamic urban institution, the role of the college union has never been more exemplified than with this project," Jeffries said. "'For students, by students,' the Student Union is a welcome and sustainable campus living room environment that values the diversity of all students."

Photos by Kristen L. Hebsrom

The former Ohio Union, opened in 1951, was one of the premier unions in its day. But over time, the building was not able to accommodate all the demands of a growing student body as event and meeting spaces were too small. After visiting newer unions at other institutions, the students of The Ohio State University decided that a new union needed to be built.

"The new Ohio Union features larger, more flexible meeting and event spaces that better meet campus needs as well as expanded the opportunities for creative programming for our Ohio Union Activities Board," Associate Director Kurtis Foriska said. "Additionally, our more than 1,000 student organizations can host events and national conferences, have office space that allows them to operate more effectively and efficiently, and have a place that is 'their' space on campus."

Branding in the Ohio Union tells the story of the union, the university, and the student leadership. A few examples of these branded concepts are: Lover's Panels featuring the names of couples that met at the university; a leadership wall that highlights student leaders; and a corridor where the doors of the university's previous unions were placed and can now be opened once again to learn the history of the individual buildings.

The Ohio Union is also a certified LEED Silver building. Green features include using local vendors, working with Habitat for Humanity during deconstruction, employing a pulping system, and creating a green tour that shows off all the sustainable aspects of the building.

"The Ohio Union's philosophy has always been that a facility is only as good as the programming and leadership that happens within its walls," Foriska said. "This new facility has expanded the opportunities to build community and young leaders in ways that seem at the forefront of what it means to be a college union."

SUBMITTED BY: Kurtis Foriska, Associate Director
FOUR-YEAR, PUBLIC, URBAN, RESIDENTIAL
FULL-TIME ENROLLMENT: 56,064
OPENED: March 29, 2010
TOTAL AREA: 318,000 sq. ft.
FLOORS: 4
ASSIGNABLE SPACE: 28%
PROJECT COST: $118 million
FUNDING SOURCE: 76% student fees, 15% institutional funding, 9% private donations
ARCHITECT: Moody-Nolan – Columbus, Ohio
FACILITIES ADDED: Branded food concepts, pub, coffee house, three quiet lounges, three television lounges, two patios, multicultural center, student organization suite, student organization storage area, information center, ticket office, two e-mail kiosks, two locker rooms, three galleries, crafts center, graphics center, copy center, retail space, spiritual room, 12 small meeting rooms, eight medium meeting rooms, 10 large meeting rooms, theater, three multipurpose rooms, administrative office space, bank, two dance rooms, instructional kitchen, and wireless Internet access

The Ohio State University (new building)
Ohio Union
Columbus, Ohio

Old Dominion University (renovation)
Lewis W. Webb University Center
Norfolk, Va.

SUBMITTED BY: Nicole Kiger, Director, Student Activities and Leadership
FOUR-YEAR, PUBLIC, RESIDENTIAL
FULL-TIME ENROLLMENT: 24,013
OPENED: 1964
REOPENED: January 2010
TOTAL AREA: 183,404 sq. ft.
AREA RENOVATED: 11,540 sq. ft.
FLOORS: 2
ASSIGNABLE SPACE: 77%
PROJECT COST: $739,326
FUNDING SOURCE: 100% student fees
ARCHITECT: Clark Nexsen – Norfolk, Va.; KSA Interiors – Richmond, Va.
FACILITIES RENOVATED: Quiet lounge, student organization suite, student organization storage area, e-mail kiosks, locker room, graphics center, small meeting room, and administrative office space
FACILITIES ADDED: Copy center, additional student organization area, two small meeting rooms, medium meeting room, and wireless Internet access

The Office of Student Activities and Leadership and the student organization offices at Old Dominion University were located on two different floors, were not big enough to accommodate the student body needs, and had not been renovated since the 1970s. It was time for a change.

A renovation at the Lewis W. Webb University Center moved the offices to one location on the first floor, making it more accessible and facilitating more interaction between staff and students.

"Once the renovation was complete, we increased the number of student organization offices available. Student organizations are now in the same space and can work and collaborate together," said Director of Student Activities and Leadership Nicole Kiger. "We witnessed involvement and use of space increase more than we originally thought possible. There is a constant crowd of students using the work tables, computers, and the offices. The students feel as if that space is 'theirs,' and they have a home in Webb Center."

The new space is in high demand among the students who would like to see it open 24 hours a day.

"We created a physical space that embodies a sense of community, collaboration, and involvement," Kiger said.

University of Rochester
Wilson Commons (renovation)
Rochester, N.Y.

SUBMITTED BY: Laura Ballou, Associate Director
FOUR-YEAR, PRIVATE, RESIDENTIAL
FULL-TIME ENROLLMENT: 5,000
OPENED: 1976
REOPENED: August 2010
AREA RENOVATED: 9,241 sq. ft.
FLOORS: 5
ASSIGNABLE SPACE: 94%
PROJECT COST: $51 million
FUNDING SOURCE: 76% institutional funding; 24% government
ARCHITECT: SWBR – Rochester, N.Y.; Beacon Architectural Associates – Boston
FACILITIES RENOVATED: Food court and games room

Since the Wilson Commons first opened on the University of Rochester campus, The Pit has served as a food court and seating area on the first floor. And while minor changes were made over the years, it was deemed that a complete renovation of the area was needed to keep up with the growth of the campus and desires of students.

The renovated area was renamed The Commons. Some improvements include new food service equipment, increase in seating area, and improved lighting. A pizza oven was added in the kitchen and a Blimpie was moved to the games room, The Hive. Additionally, many green solutions were used for the finishing touches on the renovation, such as low-VOC paint, reclaimed glass, and occupancy sensors.

The University of Rochester community is responding positively to the renovation," said Associate Director Laura Ballou. "In the first full month of operation, sales increased more than 40 percent and patron counts increased by more than 60 percent over the previous year."

University of Southern California
Ronald Tutor Campus Center (new building)
Los Angeles

SUBMITTED BY: Patrick Bailey, Senior Associate Dean of Students
FOUR-YEAR, PRIVATE
FULL-TIME ENROLLMENT: 33,500
OPENED: Aug. 23, 2010
TOTAL AREA: 194,000 sq. ft.
FLOORS: 6
ASSIGNABLE SPACE: 67%
PROJECT COST: $136 million
FUNDING SOURCE: 100% institutional funding
ARCHITECT: AC Martin Partners – Los Angeles
FACILITIES ADDED: Four branded food concepts, a snack bar, dining room, three other food services, four quiet lounges, television lounge, nightclub, two patios, student organization suite, six student organization storage areas, information center, gallery, 30 guest rooms, nine small meeting rooms, 16 medium meeting rooms, nine large meeting rooms, three theaters, multipurpose room with four sections, administrative office space, alumni office, admissions office, dining services administration office, and wireless Internet access

More than 10 years ago, it was University of Southern California students who initiated talks about a future building that "would serve as a vibrant hub for student life and all members of the Trojan Family," Senior Associate Dean of Students Patrick Bailey said. Student fees funded a study to determine the best solution for the campus. The result was the new Ronald Tutor Campus Center.

"In continuing the university's efforts to enhance the sense of community and the cocurricular experience, the goal was to construct a facility that would be the gathering place or *axis mundi* for all members of the Trojan family," Bailey said.

One stand-out feature of the new building, according to Bailey, is its art collection. With more than 100 pieces of art and Trojan memorabilia, the Art and Trojan Traditions program is able to show off the work of students, faculty, staff, alumni, and emerging artists.

Another notable claim to fame for the Campus Center is being the first LEED certified building at the university and receiving a Green Building of America Award. Some green features include filtered drinking water instead of bottled water, high-efficiency plumbing fixtures that will reduce water use by 40 percent, and a pulping system that will reduce food waste by 80 percent.

"The Ronald Tutor Campus Center has quickly established itself as the hub of activity on campus," Bailey said. "By providing space for learning beyond the classroom, the Campus Center enhances the academic life of the campus and fosters lifelong connections to the university. It has created a new definition of community at the university—one that reflects our storied history and inspires us to reach new heights as a community of learners."

State University of New York–New Paltz (renovation/addition)
Student Union
New Paltz, N.Y.

SUBMITTED BY: Michael Patterson, Director of Student Activities and Union Services
FOUR-YEAR, PUBLIC, RURAL, RESIDENTIAL
FULL-TIME ENROLLMENT: 8,000
OPENED: Sept. 1, 1971
REOPENED: Aug. 26, 2010
TOTAL AREA: 119,000 sq. ft.
AREA RENOVATED: 12,000 sq. ft.
ADDED AREA: 15,000 sq. ft.
FLOORS: 5
ASSIGNABLE SPACE: 80%
PROJECT COST: $11 million
FUNDING SOURCE: 91% government grant; 9% auxiliary services
ARCHITECT: ikon.5 architects – Princeton, N.J.
FACILITIES RENOVATED: Food service space and administrative office space
FACILITIES ADDED: Television lounge, food service space, patio, information center, e-mail kiosk, locker room, games room, small meeting room, large meeting room, general lounge, and wireless Internet access

The original Student Union at the State University of New York–New Paltz was not being utilized, and access to food service, the bookstore, and event spaces was difficult to navigate. The university set out to renovate the building to be more accommodating to the campus community.

Some changes included adding a games room, relocating the entrances to the bookstore, and moving the information center to a more visible and accessible location. Additionally, the new atrium provides a "visually stunning" addition to the building, according to Director of Student Activities and Union Services Michael Patterson.

"It breaks up the brutal architecture of the original building," he said. "Inside, the furnishings were carefully selected to create a cool and fun atmosphere for students. Students instantly embraced the addition when it opened; [it] is the place to see and be seen."

Sustainability of the renovation was a consideration during the project. Green highlights include a glass enclosure that provides daylight to 75 percent of the addition, use of lighting controls to minimize daytime energy, and use of low-VOC building materials. Also, during demolition, materials were recycled or salvaged, and new building materials came from within 500 miles of the site.

Photos courtesy of Kenneth Gabrielsen

Vanderbilt University
Sarratt Student Center (renovation)
Nashville, Tenn.

SUBMITTED BY: Jack Davis, Director, Student Centers
FOUR-YEAR, PRIVATE, URBAN, RESIDENTIAL
FULL-TIME ENROLLMENT: 6,100
OPENED: 1972
REOPENED: Aug. 20, 2010
AREA RENOVATED: 8,400 sq. ft.
FLOORS: 1
ASSIGNABLE SPACE: 100%
PROJECT COST: $500,000
FUNDING SOURCE: 100% institution funding
ARCHITECT: Gresham, Smith, and Partners – Nashville, Tenn.; Vanderbilt Campus Planning – Nashville, Tenn.
FACILITIES RENOVATED: Television lounge, patio, information center, and gallery
FACILITIES ADDED: Last Drop Coffee Shop, campus television station, and campus radio station

In May 2010, Nashville experienced historic flooding after 13 inches of rain fell in less than 24 hours. The Sarrat Student Center at Vanderbilt University was closed for a few days following the flood as much of the first floor was damaged.

"Prior to the flood, a few small projects had been considered for the first floor," said Director Jack Davis. "After the damage, our office worked with Vanderbilt Dining and the Student Communications Office to develop an overhaul of the entire public space. The goal was to create a more open, vibrant environment for students, faculty, and staff to learn and engage."

On Aug. 20, just 15 weeks later, the union reopened its newly renovated public space. Construction on the building lasted only 55 days.

"The facility upgrades include a new cafe that features Starbucks coffee, frozen yogurt, cupcakes, smoothies, wraps, and sandwiches," Davis said. "The campus television station and radio station moved to create an interactive 'fishbowl' studio. This allows the campus to watch live television and radio programs."

Photos by Steve Cross

Winthrop University (new building)
Anthony J. and Gale N. DiGiorgio Campus Center
Rock Hill, S.C.

SUBMITTED BY: Alicia R. Marstall, Director
FOUR-YEAR, PUBLIC, URBAN, RESIDENTIAL
FULL-TIME ENROLLMENT: 6,241
OPENED: September 2010
TOTAL AREA: 128,000 sq. ft.
FLOORS: 4
ASSIGNABLE SPACE: 70%
PROJECT COST: $29.4 million
FUNDING SOURCE: 100% student fees
ARCHITECT: DP3 Architect, LTD – Greenville, S.C.
FACILITIES ADDED: Five branded food concepts, coffee house, television lounge, two patios, multicultural center, student organization suite, student organization storage area, information center, ticket office, e-mail kiosk, bookstore, retail space, games room, three small meeting rooms, six medium meeting rooms, theater, multipurpose room with two sections, administrative office space, student publications, programming board office, and wireless Internet access

The old union at Winthrop University needed to be replaced. Since it opened in 1967, "things have changed on campus including the introduction of coeducation and the digital age, in addition to an increase of enrollment," said Director Alicia R. Marstall. "Another important change has been an increased focus on total student development beyond skills honed in the classroom, including cognitive, personal, and interpersonal."

The new Anthony J. and Gale N. DiGiorgio Campus Center is designed to enhance the collegiate experience, Marstall said. And the building truly gives student organizations a place to operate, offering the groups exclusive computer work stations, a conference room, storage, and mailboxes, all of which are only accessible with the appropriate university ID.

Additionally, the new Campus Center has green features including dual-pane tinted windows, artificial plastic slate shingles, recycling stations, and monitors on the air and heating units to detect the presence of people in a room.

"The addition of the DiGiorgio Campus Center has already transformed campus life in just a few short months," Marstall said. "It has quickly and seamlessly become the epicenter of campus life."

University of Wisconsin-Superior (new building)
Yellowjacket Union
Superior, Wis.

SUBMITTED BY: Gail Archambault, Director
FOUR-YEAR, PUBLIC
FULL-TIME ENROLLMENT: 2,235
OPENED: Jan. 6, 2010
TOTAL AREA: 84,600 sq. ft.
FLOORS: 2
ASSIGNABLE SPACE: 66%
PROJECT COST: $24.7 million
FUNDING SOURCE: 80% student fees; 16% private donations; 4% general purpose revenue
ARCHITECT: Workshop Architects – Milwaukee, Wis.
FACILITIES ADDED: Cafeteria, coffee house, food service area, two quiet lounges, two television lounges, patio, student organization office suite, student organization storage area, information center, three e-mail kiosks, bookstore, five medium meeting rooms, multipurpose room, administrative office space, two fireplace lounges, three interactive video gaming areas, and wireless Internet access

The University of Wisconsin–Superior's original union, the Rothwell Student Center, was built in 1959; updates over the years addressed some issues, but it was determined that the only way to meet the needs of the current campus community was to demolish the old building and rebuild.

Students were involved in the entire process, serving on the planning committee, approving architectural materials, and confirming furniture choices.

Noteworthy features, according to Director Gail Archambault, include the open spaces that allow for collaboration and the close proximity of the student organization and administrative suites that encourages interaction.

"Sustainable practices were incorporated into the design for every aspect of the project," Archambault said. "A generous roof overhang and fritted glass were specifically designed to minimize solar heat gain and reduce interior glare on bright sunny days. Directly under the roof edge is a rain garden designed to intercept overflow storm water not absorbed by the green roof. Several different species of plant materials make this area an aesthetically pleasing space while functioning as an intermittent storm water detention facility."

Additionally, Archambault said preference was given to materials composed of recycled content, were locally manufactured, and/or reduce indoor air contaminants. It is the first state-owned building in Wisconsin that was allowed to pursue official LEED certification.

"Student commitment to green, sustainable design concepts and their willingness to tax themselves to achieve these ends made this outstanding facility and its unique design features possible," Archambault said. "The excitement and pride generated by this new building has been remarkable. Participation in the community life of our campus is on the upswing. Visitor comments have been overwhelmingly positive. We love our new union."

College of Wooster (renovation)
Lowry Center
Wooster, Ohio

SUBMITTED BY: Bob Rodda, Director, Lowry Center and Student Activities
FOUR-YEAR, PRIVATE, RESIDENTIAL
FULL-TIME ENROLLMENT: 1,800
OPENED: 1968
REOPENED: Jan. 15, 2010
TOTAL AREA: 69,860 sq. ft.
AREA RENOVATED: 7,000 sq. ft.
FLOORS: 3
PROJECT COST: $400,000
FUNDING SOURCE: 100% institutional funding
ARCHITECT: MacLachan Cornelius & Filoni – Pittsburgh
FACILITIES RENOVATED: Information center, gallery, bookstore, main lounge, and post office
FACILITIES ADDED: Retail space

Realizing that a complete renovation of the Lowry Center was several years down the road, the College of Wooster decided to fast-track an update to the lower level of the building to make the space more attractive and meet students' needs in the interim.

"Goals of the project included brightening the space through the lighting, transforming the lounge into a space that would excite prospective students, and relocating the convenience store to a more secure location thereby reducing theft," Director of the Lowry Center and Student Activities Bob Rodda said.

A lounge near the coffee shop and convenience store was converted to table and chair seating for customers. The post office and information desk were combined to streamline the look and services provided. Office space was added in the bookstore, and the storage area was remodeled to increase efficiency.

"The project achieved most of its goals," Rodda said. "Use of the lounge has grown exponentially. Students are always there—studying, working in small groups, hanging out, drinking coffee, and talking to friends."

The renovation was completed in just six weeks, with the majority of construction occurring during a four-week holiday break for students.

2012

University of Connecticut

Colorado College

Minnesota State University–Mankato

Normandale Community College

Rice University

University of South Florida

University of Texas–Austin

University of Wisconsin–Madison

Western Oregon University

2012 RENOVATION & CONSTRUCTION SHOWCASE

In 2011, many institutions across the United States put the final touches on union projects. From the renovation of lounge space to expansive new buildings, these projects met the needs of the individual campus communities.

Two themes that emerged from the projects featured this year were sustainability and technology. A coffeehouse renovation at Rice University employed eco-friendly practices to compliment the sustainable goals of the student-run establishment, while the University of Wisconsin–Madison's new Union South was awarded LEED Gold certification. Keeping with the latest technology was a goal of Minnesota State University–Mankato's new "video ballroom" as well as the Sky Pad at the University of South Florida. These are just a few examples from the many presented in the showcase.

By exploring these projects, institutions considering a college union renovation or construction can learn more about the various features and approaches of the buildings included in the showcase.

RENOVATION
Rice Student Center
HOUSTON, TEXAS

RENOVATION/ADDITION
Kopp Student Center
BLOOMINGTON, MINN.

RENOVATION
Centennial Student Union
MANKATO, MINN.

169

SUBMITTED BY: Corey O'Brien, Business Manager
CAMPUS TYPE: Four-year, public, rural
FULL-TIME ENROLLMENT: 20,000
OPENED: 1952
REOPENED: September 2011
AREA RENOVATED: 5,000 sq. ft.
AREA ADDED: 10,500 sq. ft.
FLOORS: 1
ASSIGNABLE SPACE: 100%
PROJECT COST: $1.2 million
FUNDING SOURCE: 100% governmental funding
ARCHITECT: Carol Johnson and Associates – Boston
FACILITIES RENOVATED: Patio, outdoor equipment, and wireless Internet access

The University of Connecticut's Student Union renovated an outdoor space to be more useful to the campus community. "The Terrace provides a fantastic view of the Mall and invites students, faculty, staff, and guests to a quiet place to relax and enjoy our beautiful campus," Business Manager Corey O'Brien said.

The Terrace offers a much-desired alternative dining space for students as well as a place for outdoor programming such as concerts and college graduations.

"We have provided a level of event power that will enable us to create an extremely flexible program space, including recessed tie-downs to accommodate several sizes of tents," O'Brien said. "In addition, we are providing infrastructure for audio-visual support for a wide range of programs and events."

UNIVERSITY OF CONNECTICUT

RENOVATION
Student Union
STORRS, CONN.

171

SUBMITTED BY: Chris Coulter, Director of Facility Services
CAMPUS TYPE: Four-year, private, residential
FULL-TIME ENROLLMENT: 2,100
OPENED: 1965
REOPENED: Aug. 19, 2011
AREA RENOVATED: 25,344 sq. ft.
TOTAL AREA: 80,000 sq. ft.
FLOORS: 3
ASSIGNABLE SPACE: 85%
PROJECT COST: $9.5 million
FUNDING SOURCE: 100% institutional funding
ARCHITECT: Shepley Bulfinch – Boston
FACILITIES RENOVATED: Branded food concepts, cafeteria, coffee house, quiet lounge, and patio
FACILITIES ADDED: Small meeting room and broadened wireless Internet access

RENOVATION
Worner Center
COLORADO SPRINGS, COLO.

COLORADO COLLEGE

A renovation at Colorado College's Worner Center was completed in just 120 days. The project improved the eating and after-hour study functions of a dining hall space that now offers better lighting, additional power receptacles, and more Internet access points, said Director of Facility Services Chris Coulter.

"A keen focus was maintained on insuring the space met student needs first while providing the necessary durability and space flexibility to meet the intense day-to-day needs of the higher education environment," he said.

Another goal of the project was to improve the energy and water consumption of the facility. To achieve this, Energy Star kitchen equipment was purchased and a photovoltaic system was added to the rooftop. Since the renovation, according to Coulter, energy consumption has dropped 30 percent and water consumption has dropped 61 percent.

173

SUBMITTED BY: Lenny Koupal, Communications Coordinator
CAMPUS TYPE: Four-year, public, rural
FULL-TIME ENROLLMENT: 14,000
OPENED: 1967
REOPENED: October 2011
AREA RENOVATED: 31,000 sq. ft.
EXISTING AREA: 209,000 sq. ft.
FLOORS: 3
ASSIGNABLE SPACE: 100%
PROJECT COST: $4.2 million
FUNDING SOURCE: 100% student fees
ARCHITECT: Kass Wilson Architects – Minneapolis, Minn.
FACILITIES RENOVATED: Quiet lounge, multipurpose room with five sections, roof, heating and air conditioning system, and broadened wireless Internet access
FACILITIES ADDED: Ticket office

At Minnesota State University–Mankato, the Centennial Student Union now offers a unique ballroom space—referred to as a video ballroom. The renovation project updated the original ballroom from 1967. The new space utilizes technology that allows the lighting and sound to automatically adjust to changing room size, said Communications Coordinator Lenny Koupal; therefore, when any portion of the room is sectioned off, the lights and sound will still be "perfect."

"This renovation creates a first-of-its-kind video ballroom for the state of Minnesota," Koupal said. "It provides a much-needed upgrade to the last section of the original building accented by a ballroom that is now a high-efficiency, high-technology space for student and public gatherings."

A sustainable feature of the new ballroom space was the reclaiming of wood from the old ballroom. It was discovered that this wood was grown in a state pine forest that no longer exists, according to Koupal. The wood slats were used to create the main circular feature on the ceiling of the ballroom.

RENOVATION
Centennial Student Union
MANKATO, MINN.

MINNESOTA STATE UNIVERSITY–MANKATO

175

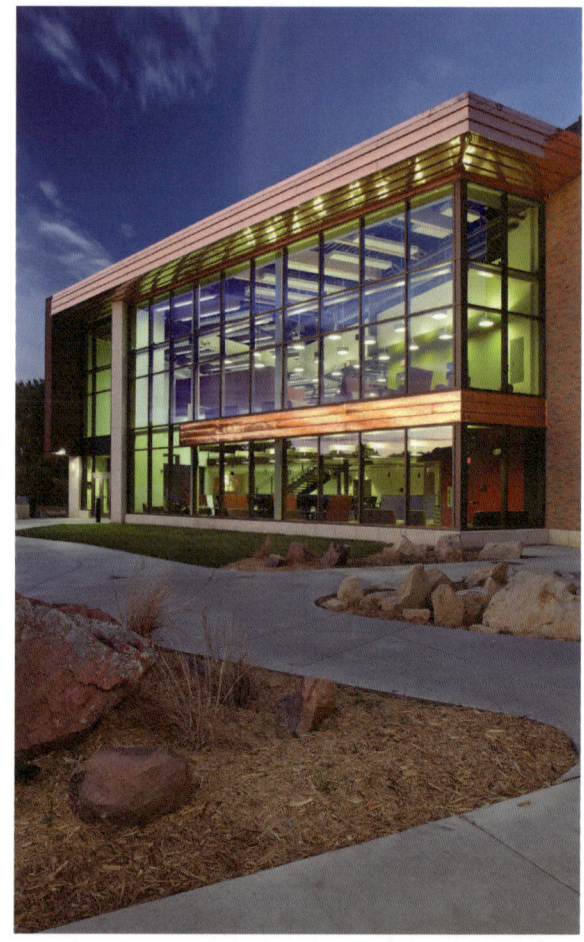

NORMANDALE
COMMUNITY COLLEGE

The Kopp Student Center originally opened in 1975, when enrollment at Normandale Community College was 3,000. Including all students, the total enrollment has tripled to 15,000.

"In the years leading up to the expansion, students would literally be sitting on the floor of the Student Center in an effort to find some place to relax, study, or socialize between classes," Director Chris Mikkelsen said. "The fact that Normandale is a commuter campus within a metropolitan area made the need for a larger Student Center important. Careful consideration to the needs of students, staff, and the community has to be made when designing a community college student center. We feel we addressed those needs and have a wonderful facility to show for it."

Noteworthy features of the renovated building include floor-to-ceiling windows that offer views of the Japanese gardens and wetland adjacent to the building. In the Overlook Lounge, a café has sushi and Japanese teas. Additionally, a tiered performance space within the lounge is wired for both live performances and movie screenings.

Students were involved in the process from approving a student fee to offering input on design features. "Their involvement is very apparent when looking at the student club and organization space," Mikkelsen said.

Sustainability was a concern throughout the project; features include using natural light, having natural light sensors in rooms, and installing a chilled beam system, which "is a type of convection heating and cooling system design to heat or cool large buildings," Mikkelsen said.

RENOVATION/ADDITION
Kopp Student Center
BLOOMINGTON, MINN.

SUBMITTED BY: Chris Mikkelsen, Director
CAMPUS TYPE: Two-year
FULL-TIME ENROLLMENT: 7,300
OPENED: 1975
REOPENED: August 2011
AREA RENOVATED: 31,735 sq. ft.
AREA ADDED: 23,375 sq. ft.
TOTAL AREA: 55,110 sq. ft.
FLOORS: 2
ASSIGNABLE SPACE: 60%
PROJECT COST: $14.5 million
FUNDING SOURCE: 75% student fees; 15% institutional funding; 10% rental and other revenue sources
ARCHITECT: LHB – Duluth, Minn.; Workshop Architects – Milwaukee, Wis.
FACILITIES RENOVATED: Two television lounges, patio, student organization space, email kiosk, gallery, and administrative office space
FACILITIES ADDED: Two snack bars, cafeteria, coffee shop, multicultural center, bookstore, retail space, one small meeting room, five medium meeting rooms, and multipurpose room with three sections

RICE UNIVERSITY

RENOVATION
Rice Student Center
HOUSTON, TEXAS

The Rice Coffeehouse is a student-run business. Before the renovation, the coffeehouse was operating in 112 sq. ft. of space. Its popularity caused long lines and traffic congestion in the Student Center, said Associate Director Pamelyn Shefman.

Even when a coffee competitor was brought on campus, the Rice Coffeehouse's customer base grew as it made "a transition to local, organic, and fair-trade products while shifting to environmentally conscious operations," Shefman said.

With a larger space, the Rice Coffeehouse now is able to be more accommodating to its customers. As it is a student-run operation, students were involved in each step of the process, including daily construction check-ins. And keeping with its sustainability focus, the coffeehouse project used eco-friendly practices such as repurposing and recycling original materials.

"This renovation, though seemingly small in many ways, speaks volumes to how Rice gets the most from its 'smallness,'" Shefman said.

SUBMITTED BY: Pamelyn Shefman, Associate Director
CAMPUS TYPE: Four-year, private, urban, residential
FULL-TIME ENROLLMENT: 5,275
OPENED: 1958
REOPENED: 2011
AREA RENOVATED: 1,947 sq. ft.
FLOORS: 3
ASSIGNABLE SPACE: 100%
PROJECT COST: $284,500
FUNDING SOURCE: 59% institutional funding; 20.7% coffeehouse; 19.5% Student Center
ARCHITECT: Intexture Architects – Houston
FACILITIES RENOVATED: Coffeehouse

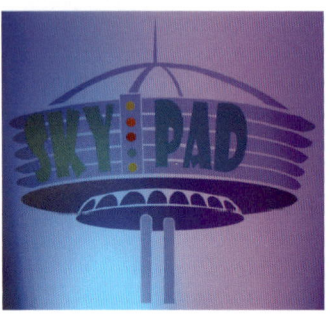

SUBMITTED BY: Jen Hernandez, Associate Director
CAMPUS TYPE: Four-year, public, urban
FULL-TIME ENROLLMENT: 45,000
OPENED: August 2008
REOPENED: September 2011
AREA RENOVATED: 2,750 sq. ft.
TOTAL AREA: 235,000 sq. ft.
FLOORS: 4
PROJECT COST: $430,000
FUNDING SOURCE: Auxiliary fund
ARCHITECT: Gould Evans Associates – Tampa, Fla.

The University of South Florida converted two meeting rooms on the Fourth Floor of the Marshall Student Center into the Sky Pad, "a student lounge complete with a gaming room," said Associate Director Jen Hernandez.

Features of the Sky Pad included futuristic-style furniture, study area with two study pods, a whiteboard wall, and a vending area. According to Hernandez, each study pod boasts a LCD screen that students are able to plug into and work on group projects.

A separated gaming area in the Sky Pad offers five gaming pods with LCD screens and overhead cone speakers that provide directional sound.

"The lounge is a hit with both gamers and students looking for a place to study and relax," Hernandez said. "The Sky Pad has seating for approximately 90 students and is one of the busiest spots for students in

RENOVATION
Marshall Student Center
TAMPA, FLA.

UNIVERSITY OF SOUTH FLORIDA

181

SUBMITTED BY: Crystal King, Student Activity Center Director
CAMPUS TYPE: Four-year, public, urban
FULL-TIME ENROLLMENT: 50,000
OPENED: Dec. 16, 2010
TOTAL AREA: 149,000 sq. ft.
FLOORS: 6
ASSIGNABLE SPACE: 66%
PROJECT COST: $68 million
FUNDING SOURCE: 70% student fees; 30% institutional funding
ARCHITECT: WTW Architects – Pittsburgh; Overland Partner Architects – San Antonio
FACILITIES ADDED: Four branded food concepts, two quiet lounges, four patios, multicultural center, student organization storage area, information center, ticket office, locker room, gallery, spiritual area, one small meeting room, five medium meeting rooms, two large meeting rooms, three theaters, multipurpose room with two sections, administrative offices, and wireless Internet access

UNIVERSITY OF TEXAS–AUSTIN

For more than 50 years, students at the University of Texas–Austin have been dreaming of a union that could better meet their needs. And the growing student population only added to the woes of the previously undersized building.

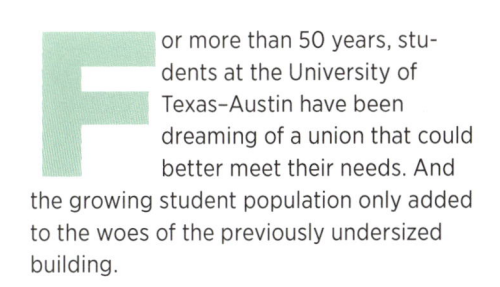

According to Student Activity Center Director Crystal King, students were involved with the new building from the start. During one portion of planning, students were put into teams and asked to create the building they desired.

A key feature of the new building is more than 25,000 sq. ft. of outdoor space, which, said King, resulted from value engineering and includes water features, decks, lighting, electrical, and tree canopies.

"Our students led the charge in building the facility and remained active in the process over many years," she said. "The Student Activity Center is a college union that represents the needs and desires of the current student."

NEW BUILDING
Student Activity Center
AUSTIN, TEXAS

183

SUBMITTED BY: Marc Kennedy, Communications Director
CAMPUS TYPE: Four-year, public, urban, residential
FULL-TIME ENROLLMENT: 42,099
OPENED: April 15, 2011
TOTAL AREA: 200,000 sq. ft.
FLOORS: 5
ASSIGNABLE SPACE: 67%
PROJECT COST: $94 million
FUNDING SOURCE: 100% student fees
ARCHITECT: Workshop Architects – Milwaukee, Wis.; Moody Nolan – Columbus, Ohio
FACILITIES ADDED: Three branded food concepts, two snack bars, pub, coffee shop, quiet lounge, two television lounges, a nightclub, four patios, two student organization suites, information center, ticket office, two email kiosks, locker room, gallery, retail space, eight bowling lanes, one games room, spiritual area, 60 guest rooms, two small meeting rooms, 11 medium meeting rooms, three large meeting rooms, theater, a multipurpose room with three sections, administrative offices, visitor's center, credit union, campus ID services, and wireless Internet access

NEW BUILDING
Union South
MADISON, WIS.

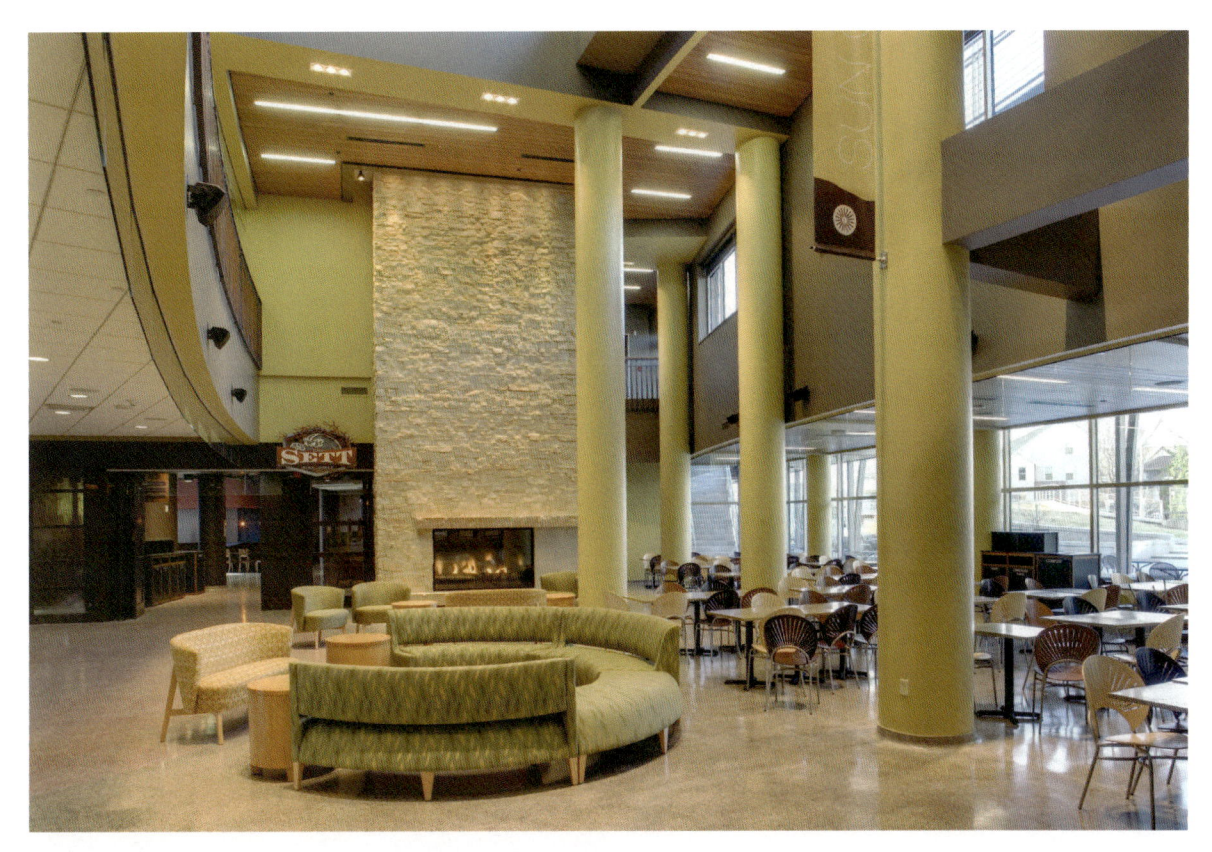

University of Wisconsin–Madison's original Union South was built more than 30 years ago and was no longer adequately serving the campus community. Students indicated the need for a new, sustainable building that would draw in the campus community and offer an array of services not currently available, according to Communications Director Marc Kennedy.

Noteworthy features of the new building include a nightclub, climbing wall, large meeting spaces, updated audio-visual equipment, and a green roof, which is not the only sustainable element. Union South was honored with a LEED Gold certification for recycling nearly 90 percent of the original building materials, using regional materials in the new building when possible, and using natural light to reduce energy needs, among other features.

"Students got what they demanded and paid for—a warm, inviting 'people magnet,' equipped with the latest technology that offers an array of services concomitant with a 21st century student union that adheres to the design team's original philosophy of sustainability, student involvement, and creating community," Kennedy said. "The proof is in the building's immediate popularity."

UNIVERSITY OF WISCONSIN-MADISON

After analyzing facility usage, Western Oregon University decided some changes needed to be made in the Werner University Center.

"It was determined that all student lounge and community areas were on the interior of the facility with little or no access to light," said Director Jon Tucker. "We also really wanted to have the Multicultural Student Services and Programs Office relocated to the Werner University Center—the heart of campus."

Students were involved from start to finish with the renovation project. A key feature, according to Tucker, is a window wall overlooking campus from the new lounge/multipurpose smart conference room.

"We are a small school that doesn't have opportunities to remodel very often," Tucker said. "We took a relatively small project and created something that is of high value to the university and helps us start achieving a culture shift for an aging facility."

SUBMITTED BY: Jon Tucker, Director
CAMPUS TYPE: Four-year, public, rural
FULL-TIME ENROLLMENT: 6,200
OPENED: 1960
REOPENED: October 2011
AREA RENOVATED: 14,000 sq. ft.
AREA ADDED: 3,000 sq. ft.
TOTAL AREA: 79,500 sq. ft.
FLOORS: 2
ASSIGNABLE SPACE: 65%
PROJECT COST: $2 million
FUNDING SOURCE: 100% student fees
ARCHITECT: Soderstrom Architects, Ltd. – Portland, Ore.
FACILITIES RENOVATED: Multicultural office, administrative office space, and broadened wireless Internet access
FACILITIES ADDED: Coffee shop, quiet lounge, and student organization storage space

Photos not available.

RENOVATION/ADDITION
Werner University Center
MONMOUTH, ORE.

WESTERN OREGON UNIVERSITY